Comparing Cultures

A Cooperative Approach to a Multicultural World

Revised Edition

John W. Pickering

J. WESTON
WALCH
PUBLISHER

Portland, Maine

Photo Credits

Pages 19, 21	Tiziana and Gianni Baldizzone/Corbis
Pages 85, 87	Corel Corp.
All others	John W. Pickering

User's Guide
to
Walch Reproducible Books

As part of our general effort to provide educational materials which are as practical and economical as possible, we have designated this publication a "reproducible book." The designation means that purchase of the book includes purchase of the right to limited reproduction of all pages on which this symbol appears:

Here is the basic Walch policy: We grant to individual purchasers of this book the right to make sufficient copies of reproducible pages for use by all students of a single teacher. This permission is limited to a single teacher, and does not apply to entire schools or school systems, so institutions purchasing the book should pass the permission on to a single teacher. Copying of the book or its parts for resale is prohibited.

Any questions regarding this policy or requests to purchase further reproduction rights should be addressed to:

Permissions Editor
J. Weston Walch, Publisher
321 Valley Street • P. O. Box 658
Portland, Maine 04104-0658

Contents

Unit II: Creating a New Culture 97

Foreword

The materials in this book were developed because of my desire to engage students personally, as well as intellectually, in the study of other cultures. The materials are drawn largely from my readings about Bolivia and Ghana, and from my travels in the Maritime Provinces of Canada, the republics of Russia and Georgia, the Australian state of Tasmania, and South Korea. The methods and content have undergone considerable revision from year to year as I have used them with students and as other colleagues who have used them have discussed with me more effective methods of presentation.

This third edition of *Comparing Cultures* supplies current information about the history and customs of peoples featured in the earlier editions. Additional resources and activities deepen the treatment of these cultures. In addition, families in two more countries, Ghana and Tasmania, have been added so as to feature a culture on each inhabited continent. The explosion of learning opportunities from the World Wide Web also has prompted a new feature in *Comparing Cultures:* the inclusion of relevant World Wide Web and E-mail addresses.

Special thanks go to Craig Dickinson of Woodpile Inc. of Wells, Maine, and Beth Smith of Samuel L. Wagner School in Winterport, Maine, for their invaluable help in the earlier stages of this writing. I am indebted to Dr. Edward Brazee of the University of Maine for his suggestions regarding adapting the material for use in a middle-school setting. I wish also to thank my students at the Asa C. Adams school in Orono, Maine, and my students at the University of Maine College of Education for the ideas I received from their enthusiastic creation of new cultures.

I am grateful to my mother-in-law, Mildred Carson, for her numerous proofreadings of the manuscript.

My deepest gratitude goes to my wife, Marisue, whose patient and competent editing were combined with her ever-present support during the entire writing process.

To the Teacher

Many educators have called for new curricula that would capitalize on the unique nature of the early adolescent learner. It was with this need in mind that *Comparing Cultures* was designed.

Comparing Cultures is an approach to learning based on the following understanding of young adolescent development:

- Students in young adolescence (10–15) are engaged in a process of social definition that takes them from childhood dependence to greater freedom and responsibility.

- Students undergo major biological changes that alter their behavior with others.

- Students entering young adolescence are developing the ability to think more abstractly about ideas and concepts, to reflect on their own behaviors and thoughts, and to weigh conflicting values.

- Students move through young adolescence at very different rates.

Comparing Cultures uses several methods to meet the following educational needs of the young adolescent:

- The need to work cooperatively with peers;

- The need to work at one's own intellectual and social development level, and to have that contribution valued;

- The need for learning activities that enable students to integrate experiences and material;

- The need to conduct independent inquiry and then to share and evaluate the results of that inquiry.

Three of the teaching methods used in *Comparing Cultures* are of particular importance. They are discussed on the following page.

Integration of Social Studies and Language Arts Materials and Classes

Comparing Cultures can be used with great success by social studies or language arts teachers working independently or by teachers from both subject areas working cooperatively. Materials developed by the students involved in this curriculum project could be the subject of language arts lessons on mechanics, syntax, theme development, and process writing, as well as numerous other topics.

There is ample opportunity for teachers of both subjects to use children's literature about or from each culture. Stories could be integrated in various ways.

With careful planning, colleagues in science and math also can find ways to use the materials. Social science concepts and methods—such as learning historical background, assessing the role of the physical environment, using social science terminology, and learning through small-group interaction—are used throughout the entire project. For each culture studied, many language arts techniques and materials—such as creative writing, journal writing, storytelling, dramatics, and historical fiction—are suggested.

Development of Cooperative Learning Groups

Students will work together in cooperative learning groups to accomplish many of the tasks set forth in *Comparing Cultures*. In these small, mixed-ability groups, students study the various cultures, compare foreign cultures with their own, and create their own small-group culture. They can also use the groups as a laboratory for studying their own cultural similarities and differences.

Utilization of Student and Teacher Resources and Interests

Both students and teachers bring their own experiences and interests to the material treated in *Comparing Cultures*. These can be used to expand the knowledge of the different cultures. Teachers can add their own materials to expand the information about a particular culture, or they can substitute an entirely different culture with which they are more familiar. Students can be encouraged to describe their prior experience with a culture or conduct their own inquiry into topics that interest them. Both students and teachers can be on the lookout for ways to pose new questions, make generalizations, and expand the focus of the specific material provided.

How to Use This Book

This volume is designed and sold by its author and publisher as a reproducible book. Buyers have the right to photocopy or otherwise duplicate student pages in quantity sufficient for all students in all classes of a single teacher. These pages are identified as *exercises* and are located at the end of each activity.

During their use of *Comparing Cultures,* students will need to refer to the exercise pages. Before beginning use of those pages, therefore, insure that students are equipped with notebooks or inexpensive folders for filing the pages.

More detailed information about how to structure the cooperative learning groups, how to evaluate students' work, and where to read more about collaborative learning is provided in Cooperative Learning, the second section of Unit I.

UNIT I

Learning About
World Cultures

Unit I: Learning About New Cultures

An Overview

This unit has two major goals: (1) to compare and contrast three to seven widely diverse cultures and (2) to identify factors influencing cultural development. Students begin by studying their own culture and continue by investigating two to six specific families from different geographic locations and historical periods. Students also will learn certain social science concepts needed in comparing and contrasting the various cultures.

The success of this unit depends on the teacher's willingness to promote certain attitudes that facilitate student learning. First, teachers need genuinely to accept values and practices that differ from their own. This acceptance will enable students to view the members of another culture as individuals from whom they can learn valuable lessons.

Second, teachers need to communicate to students that the causes of cultural diversity are multiple and that any answer to the question "Why do they do this?" can provide only a partial explanation. Nevertheless, students can look at a cultural difference and seek to identify some of the factors that have led to a particular practice.

Although Unit I (Learning About World Cultures) is designed to precede Unit II (Creating a New Culture), the units can be used independently. They can be used successfully in grades five through eight, with the teacher reading aloud some of the more difficult material to the lower-grade students.

Unit I will be most effective if done on consecutive days until the unit is completed. The time needed to complete the unit will depend on the number of cultures studied and the degree to which both the supplementary and the language arts materials are used. Under normal circumstances, each culture can be covered in a minimum of three class sessions. Maximum benefit can be derived if adequate time is given to comparing and contrasting the cultures and to seeking the multiple reasons for their differences.

Cooperative Learning

Cooperative learning groups are used extensively throughout the two units of *Comparing Cultures*. Therefore, some comments are needed about how to structure these groups, how to support students as they work in cooperative learning groups, and how to assess and evaluate their progress. It is highly recommended that you select one of the books listed in the bibliography in order to become even more skillful in using cooperative learning in your classroom.

For students to derive the greatest benefit from working together, many components should be present. (1) Students should work together in ways that make them interdependent. This can be accomplished by having them share limited resources, solve a problem that cannot be completed until all students have done their part of the work, or teach each other a skill they have learned that the group needs. (2) Students should be expected to learn some of the social skills required to work together. Specific skills—like listening, taking turns, criticizing ideas rather than people, accepting differences, contributing ideas, managing materials, and others—can be taught and practiced as part of their group assignment. (3) Individual students should be held accountable for meeting the learning objectives. Work with others is done to help them all master the material, so no student should be exempt from full engagement in learning. (4) Each time they work together, students should be given the opportunity to process what they have done. They should discuss their academic and social skill learning in terms of what went well, what hindered the group's progress, and what could be done differently next time.

Both units in the book lend themselves to having students work in mixed-ability groups. They contain numerous opportunities for students to share opinions and ample values activities to which all students can contribute on an equal basis. The reading and writing tasks require that one or more members of the group be at a sixth-grade reading and writing level or higher. This provides an opportunity for peer teaching and pair work, which should be taken into account when the groups are assigned.

When students are working to construct their own culture, there are opportunities for them to select tasks that meet their particular interest and skill level, again providing a chance for students to experience all members of their group as equal partners. Sensitivity to the different needs and continual molding of the task to the group are most helpful.

When students work together in groups, assessment and evaluation need to fit the type of task done. It is entirely appropriate to have pencil and paper tests for some of the material learned and to assign grades to individual students based on how well they learned that material. However, when it comes to assessing the work that students do on their cultures, the task becomes more complex. Traditional testing becomes more difficult; therefore, several alternative assessment approaches are suggested.

1. A variety of response formats is appropriate for students working in groups— things like performances, group interviews, individual written logs, and artwork. In this way each student's contribution, as well as the total quality of the group's product, can be assessed.

2. A well-designed checklist can be used to assess the growth students make in their interpersonal and group process skills. Three category levels can be designated: has the knowledge, applies the knowledge, and reflects on the use of the knowledge. If assigning a grade seems inappropriate, then a reporting form could be devised to help each student look at his/her growth over a period of time.

3. An assessment of the products of each group can be made as long as a set of standards has been clearly developed and students know what those standards are. It is most desirable to have students decide that they wish to have their own grade be the same as that assigned to the group product, because without that decision, issues of fairness regarding who did more work on the product tend to make the assessment a negative experience for all participants. If there is not that assent, students can be asked to supply a piece of their own work for the group for assessment as their contribution to that project.

4. Many books treat assessment of performance-based learning. The approach taken by *A Teacher's Guide to Performance-Based Learning and Assessment* (Pomperaug Regional School District 15), listed in the Cooperative Learning Bibliography, would be particularly beneficial to use in conjunction with the cooperative learning activities suggested in *Comparing Cultures*.

Bibliography

Cohen, Elizabeth. *Designing Groupwork: Strategies for the Heterogeneous Classroom.* 2d ed. New York: Teachers College Press, 1994.

Educators in Connecticut's Pomperaug Regional School District 15. *A Teacher's Guide to Performance-Based Learning and Assessment.* Alexandria, VA: ASCD, 1996.

Hill, Susan, and Tom Hill. *The Collaborative Classroom.* Portsmouth, NH: Heinemann, 1990.

Johnson, David, and Roger Johnson. *Meaningful and Manageable Assessment through Cooperative Learning.* Edina, MN: Interaction Book Co., 1996.

Johnson, David, Roger Johnson, and Edythe Hollubec. *Teaching Students to Be Peacemakers, Third Edition.* Edina, MN: Interaction Book Co., 1995.

_____. *The New Circles of Learning.* Alexandria, VA: ASCD, 1994.

Kagan, Spencer. *Cooperative Learning.* Rev. ed. San Clemente, CA: Kagan Cooperative Learning, 1997.

Reid, Jo-Anne, Peter Forrestal, and Jonathan Cook. *Small Group Learning in the Classroom.* Portsmouth, NH: Heinemann, 1991.

Rottier, Jerry, and Beverly Ogan. *Cooperative Learning in Middle Level Schools.* Washington, DC: NEA Professional Library, National Education Association, 1991.

Slavin, Robert. *Student Team Learning: A Practical Guide to Cooperative Learning.* Washington, DC: NEA Professional Library, National Education Association, 1991.

Widerholt, Chuck. *Cooperative Learning and Higher Level Thinking: The Question Matrix.* Rev. ed. San Clemente, CA: Kagan Cooperative Learning, 1994.

Activity 1. Getting Started

Introduction

Students are introduced to the tasks required in Unit I and acquainted with specific terms used by social scientists to describe different aspects of a culture.

Objectives

1. To give students an understanding of the overall structure of Unit I

2. To teach students specific terms used by social scientists in studying cultures

Time to complete

One class period

Materials

- Exercise 1: Terms and Definitions Relating to Culture

Procedure

1. Divide the class into cooperative learning groups of three or four students each. It is best that students be placed in groups that have a balanced mix of boys and girls, academic abilities, and personalities. Prior experience in working with others in a group should also be taken into consideration. Because many of the students' learning experiences will occur in these cooperative learning groups, it is useful to explain to students why this kind of learning group is used and how it works. Students should understand that a significant amount of their learning in this

project will come from their work with each other, thus necessitating a serious attitude toward the cooperative learning group.

When given tasks to do in cooperative learning groups, the students work in the groups during the class period. They may pair up during part of the time or work all together on a task. The goal is to get all students involved in the cooperative work, so you may need to intervene to help integrate members who have difficulty getting involved.

Students may be moved from one group into another if such a change would help them work more effectively with each other.

2. You might wish to push desks together to give students a common working surface and to facilitate communication.

3. Explain to the students what they will be doing during this unit. Tell them that they will be both looking at their own culture and studying the lives of families from other cultures.

4. Explain that social scientists use terms and concepts as tools to understand different social phenomena, so they, too, will need to acquire these tools in order to study different cultures.

5. Give out to each student a copy of Exercise 1: Terms and Definitions Relating to Culture.

6. In class, explain each term and make sure it is clearly understood. Supplement some of the examples from the handout with others from contemporary culture, if helpful.

7. Have students in each group orally quiz each other on the meanings of the terms.

8. Finish the class session with a short, oral question-and-answer session to reinforce the meaning of the terms.

Exercise 1

Terms and Definitions
Relating to Culture

Culture: The way of life of a group of people.

Traditions, customs, values, and the level of technology are all part of a culture.

Customs: Special practices that are common to one group of people.

Examples would be the way people wear their hair, what clothes they wear, and what kind of transportation they use.

Traditions: Customs that survive from one generation to the next generation.

Examples would be religious celebrations, festivals and national holidays, and rituals, such as how a culture deals with a child's baby tooth falling out.

Technology: The scientific knowledge and tools available to a culture.

The more complex and diverse the knowledge and tools, the higher the level of technology.

Technology ranges from the hoe to the space shuttle.

Values: Beliefs about what is good, desirable, and worth holding on to.

What we do and what we say are based on values.

Values can be held by many people at the same time. Schooling for all children is an example of a value.

Activity 2. Your Own Culture

Introduction

A starting point for understanding differences among cultures is a study of the major practices within one's own culture. Typical customs, ideas, and behaviors are first identified so they can later be investigated.

Objectives

1. To have students describe in a class discussion major features of their culture

2. To have students list the major features of their own culture

3. To develop students' ability to identify customs, traditions, values, and technology of their own culture

Time to complete

Two class periods

Materials

• Exercise 2: Your Own Culture

Procedure

1. Explain to the students that they will be asked to give typical examples for each listed feature of their culture. *Typical* should be interpreted as that which would be practiced most frequently by families represented in the classroom. When an

example is given that is judged not to be typical, it may provide an opportunity to discuss different practices.

2. Give each student Exercise 2: Your Own Culture.

3. As a class, come up with examples for each feature listed on the worksheet. Write them on the blackboard, allowing time for students to copy them onto their worksheet. They will use this worksheet (and others) to compare and contrast individual practices of each culture

4. Pause occasionally so that students can identify the social science term that applies to a particular practice in their culture. For example, when people vote for a representative, they are doing something that their culture believes is valuable (a *value*), whereas it is customary (a *custom*) in the Altiplano region of Bolivia to make men's hats from llama's wool.

5. The entire exercise is enhanced if students are talking about examples and sharing their own cultural experiences. Care must be taken to remain on task yet still be aware of the richness in students' stories.

6. An alternative approach to recording what is typical is to have students work in the cooperative learning groups to generate ideas which are then recorded on each group member's worksheet. This will work best when students have had prior experience working together in cooperative groups.

Exercise 2

Your Own Culture

Food	**Rules and Penalties**
Clothing	**Type of Government**
Housing	**Transportation**
Language	**Education**
Religion	**Other Special Features**

Activity 3. Aymara Family

Introduction

The Aymara Indian family described in this material is a real contemporary family in La Paz, Bolivia. The Aymara is one of several cultural groups in Bolivia, others being Quechua Indian and peoples of mixed European and native ancestry. Although each of the cultural groups has different customs, Bolivia as a country has certain practices that all groups share. Make sure students understand that a country can have several cultural groups living together at the same time.

Objectives

1. To have students discover and record the major features of the culture of the Aymara family living in La Paz, Bolivia

2. To develop students' ability to identify in another culture examples of customs, traditions, values, and technology

Time to complete

A minimum of three class periods

Materials

- Exercise 3: Map of Bolivia
- Exercise 4: Aymara Family—Cultural Features
- Exercise 5: Letter to a Sister
- Exercise 6: Report from a Health Center Doctor

Procedure

1. Locate La Paz, Bolivia, on the class map and list specific details of altitude, climate, ties to other regions of Bolivia, latitude, and longitude. Have students suggest ways in which these factors might affect the culture of people living in this area. Point out large cities, natural features, and latitude and longitude. Have students add these to their map in Exercise 3.

2. Distribute Exercise 4: Aymara Family—Cultural Features. Make sure students understand that each of the listed items is an important feature to look for and assess in understanding any culture.

   Read to the class Exercise 5: Letter to a Sister. Have students select examples from the letter that exemplify each cultural feature listed in Exercise 4. Write these examples on the blackboard, and make sure students copy them on Exercise 4.

3. An alternative approach would be to have students read the letter aloud in their cooperative learning groups and individually record examples of each feature on Exercise 4.

4. Repeat either procedure 2 or 3 for Exercise 6: Report from a Health Center Doctor.

5. If there is little available information about a particular cultural feature, have each group of students conduct library research to supply the remaining information. Social studies textbooks on Bolivia or an encyclopedia should supply the necessary information. Additional research can be conducted using some of the books and Web sites suggested in the bibliography at the end of the Aymara Family section.

6. Write on the blackboard the following social science terms: *custom, tradition, value,* and *technology.* Ask students to cite examples of each one from the Aymara culture.

7. Have each small group list the five practices in the Aymara culture that seem most different from those of their own culture. Have each group use these five practices as the basis for a travel poster designed to attract tourists to La Paz, Bolivia. When the students have finished their posters, have them share their creations with the other groups.

Suggestions for Further Study of the Aymara Culture

- Have students study about the arrival of the Spanish conquistadores in South America. Then have them create a drama showing the cultural clash between the Spaniards and the Aymara Indians.

- La Paz is at an elevation of 12,000 feet. Ask students to suggest ways in which the body is affected by that altitude. Then ask if any students are interested in making a report on the effects of high altitude on the human body.

- Have students do research to discover the kinds of clothing that must be worn in high altitudes.

- Read Ann Nolan Clark's book *Secret of the Andes*. Compare the life and customs of the main character (Cusi) to those of Constancia's family in La Paz.

Resource Information About Bolivia

- Bolivia has a population of approximately 8 million people. La Paz, the capital, has a population of 711,000. More than half the population is under 20 years of age. Life expectancy is 60 years for men and 65 years for women. Birth rates are high, and death rates are particularly high for young children. Aymara and Quechua Indians make up about half the population; another third are of mixed European and native ancestry, and the rest are of European descent. The Roman Catholic religion is practiced by 90 percent of the population. About 85 percent of the population is literate.

- Located just above the Tropic of Capricorn, Bolivia has a tropical rain forest in the northeast, a large high interior basin in the southwest (the Altiplano), and two major mountain ranges running on either side of the Altiplano. Elevations on the Altiplano run from 12,000 to 15,000 feet, with the highest mountain, Nevado Illampu (21,000 feet), located a few miles from La Paz.

- La Paz, the administrative capital of Bolivia, is the site for the meeting of the National Congress, which is composed of the 102-member Chamber of Deputies and a 27-member Senate. The president and cabinet are elected through popular elections, although this is a fairly recent development. Previous to popular elections, Bolivia went through a succession of mostly military leaders. Sucre, the judicial capital, is the site for the meeting of the 12-member supreme court. The country of Bolivia is divided into 9 departments and 112 provinces.

- Bolivia is an extremely poor country, with only 3 percent of its land arable; of this land, 50 percent is cultivated and 25 percent is used as pasture. Cattle, sheep, goats, and pigs, as well as llama and alpaca, are raised. About 25 inches of rain falls in the La Paz area, with about 70 inches falling in the northeastern tropics. Copper and tin are mined in the mountains. There are few paved roads and minimal rail transportation.

Bibliography

Blair, David Nelson. *The Land and People of Bolivia*. New York: Harper Collins, 1990. (Children's literature)

————. *Fear the Condor*. New York: Lodestar Books (Dutton Children's Books), 1992. (Children's literature)

Buchler, Hans, and Judith Buchler. *The Bolivian Aymara*. New York: Holt Rinehart and Winston, 1971.

Clark, Ann. *Secret of the Andes*. New York: Viking Penguin, 1987. (Children's literature)

Cramer, Mark. *Bolivia: Culture Shock*. Portland, OR: Graphic Arts Center Publishing Co., 1996.

Delacre, Lulu. *Senor Cat's Romance and Other Favorite Stories From Latin America*. New York: Scholastic, 1997. (Children's literature)

Deltenre, Chantal, and Martine Noblet. *Tintin's Travel Diaries: Peru and the Andean Countries*. Hauppauge, NY: Barron's Educational Series, Inc., 1995. (Children's literature)

Dunkerley, James. *Rebellion in the Veins*. Norfolk, England: Thetford Press, 1984.

Griffiths, John. *Let's Visit Bolivia*. London: Burke Publishers, 1987. (Children's literature)

Klein, Herbert. *Bolivia: The Evolution of a Multiethnic Society*. New York: Oxford University Press, 1992.

Lerner Publications, Department of Geography Staff, ed. *Bolivia in Pictures*. Minneapolis: Lerner Publications, 1987. (Children's literature)

Martin, Michael, ed. *Children of the World: Bolivia*. Milwaukee: Gareth Stevens Publishers, 1988. (Children's literature)

McEwen, William. *Changing Rural Society: A Study of Communities in Bolivia*. New York: Oxford University Press, 1975.

St. John, Jetty. *A Family in Bolivia*. Milwaukee: Gareth Stevens Publishers, 1988. (Children's literature)

Schimmel, Karen. *Bolivia*. New York: Chelsea House, a Division of Main Line Book Company, 1991. (Children's literature)

Swaney, Deanna. *Bolivia: Lonely Planet Travel Survival Kit*. Oakland, CA: Lonely Planet Publications, 1996.

World Wide Web

http://www.cs.purdue.edu/homes/krsul/bolivia/
   (Excellent—very up to date, many connections)

http://www.astro.uva.nl/michielb/bolivia.html

http://www.lonelyplanet.com.au/dest/sam/bolivia.htm

http://www.main.nc.us/ARHC/
   (Andean Rural Healthcare)

http://travel.yahoo.com/Destinations/South_America/Countries/Bolivia/
   (General site with many connections)

E-mail

bolivia@cs.purdue.edu

Exercise 3

Map of Bolivia

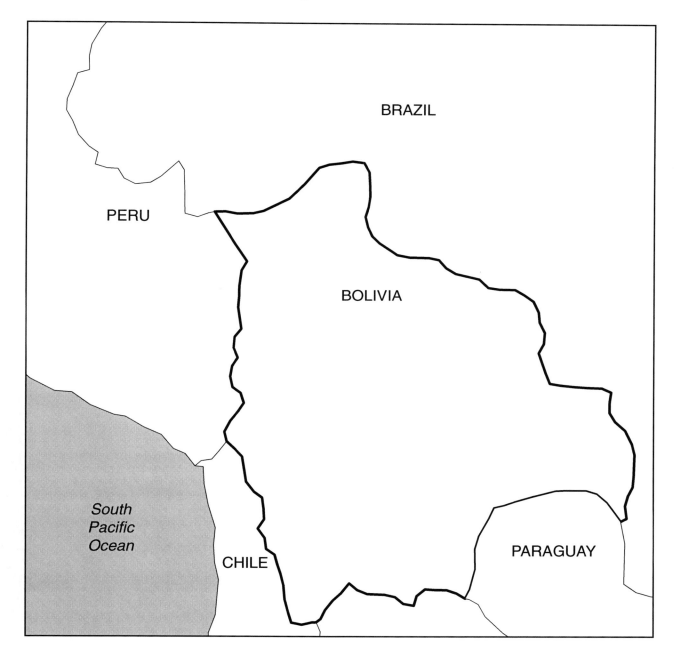

Exercise 4

Aymara Family—Cultural Features

Food	Rules and Penalties
Clothing	Type of Government
Housing	Transportation
Language	Education
Religion	Other Special Features

Comparing Cultures

Exercise 5

Letter to a Sister

La Paz, Bolivia

January 15

Dear Paulina,

I miss you very much. I wish I were old enough to come to Tambillo to work on the farm with you. Are you weeding the potatoes and carrots, or does Uncle Alberto have you tending the llamas and sheep? I would rather tend the llamas, but I don't think I would like to feel the constantly blowing wind on the Altiplano.

In your last letter you described the celebration that was held when the community center was finished. I especially liked how you told about the folk dancing with the drums and flutes playing. We haven't had a celebration here for some time, so I am looking forward to Carnival so I can dress up in my special costume. Mother is making me a new skirt and sweater and is making Edgar a poncho. He'll look grown up, don't you think?

Bolivian women gathered for the festival

This morning before Father caught the bus for Villa Tajedae, where he is working on a house, he talked to me again about how important going to school is. He would like to be able to have more steady work than he is able to get as a carpenter, but he knows that his lack of schooling has kept him from getting a higher-paying job. I want to do well in school. I worry that Father and Mother won't have enough money to send me to intermediate school. I'm sorry they weren't able to send you to high school; I know you were looking forward to being a teacher.

Yesterday Mother was talking about how few potatoes and tomatoes she is able to get to sell in the market. The drought has hurt all the crops badly. It would be good if you could hurry along the crop of potatoes you are growing.

(continued)

Exercise 5

Letter to a Sister *(continued)*

Since you moved to Tambillo, I have had to do more work at home. I don't mind getting the water every morning at the community tap, because I can visit with Maria. I do hate whitewashing our adobe walls, though. The whitewash soaks in so fast it seems to take forever. I'm glad nothing needs to be done on our tin roof. I hate heights, even of just one story!

I've been playing a game with Edgar, and part of the game includes having him sweep the dirt floor. Mother told me that I had to do that job, but I figure if I can get Edgar to do it, I will have more time to cook for her while she is selling her vegetables.

I went to the public health clinic the other day to get my diphtheria shot. The doctor was nice and asked me all kinds of questions about everyone in our family. He asked about what we ate and then told me we should try to get more protein. I know he is right, but it is hard when meat and fish are so expensive. I think that is why mother feels so weak all the time. It worries me that she has to leave so early in the morning to sell vegetables in the market.

Maria and I went to downtown La Paz last week. I like looking at all the tall buildings and seeing the cars and buses go by. I looked at a newspaper headline concerning our elections. I hope we can continue to elect our president. Father says our country is much better off than when the military was in control. He is afraid there will be another attempt to get rid of the president, though, because there are so many problems. Too many people are trying to come to live in La Paz. Father says that is one of the reasons he is having such a hard time getting work as a carpenter.

Mother has been saving up money for over a month so we can have *empanada saltena*. She is allowing me to fix it for the first time. I remember that it was one of your favorite meals. I already have the chicken and meat cooked, so I can add the potatoes, olives, and peppers as soon as I finish this letter. I hope I don't have trouble getting the dough fried. This is one of my favorite foods because I like wrapping the dough around all the other things. Edgar looks funny eating it, with tears coming down his face. He isn't used to food that hot.

I must stop writing and send this to you.

Love,

Constancia

20   *Comparing Cultures*

Name _____   Date _____

Exercise 6

Report from a Health Center Doctor

La Paz Central Health Clinic

January 12

Report on Visit of Constancia Garcia

On January 10 Constancia Garcia visited the health clinic for a diphtheria shot. In addition to the shot, I took a family history, in order to gain information that will better enable us to meet the medical needs of this family.

Bolivian street scene

As with most people living in this section of La Paz, the Garcias have trouble with proper sanitation. The water from the public tap is vastly cleaner than it was, but there is still some concern that it causes much sickness. Constancia told me that her mother is often sick and has to miss selling vegetables in the market. Constancia reports that her family is aware of the need to keep things clean in order to remain healthy.

Constancia suffers from mild malnutrition due to a high-carbohydrate, low-protein diet. Her daily intake of calories is not sufficient to enable her to develop a strong body. The family relies mainly on potatoes for their daily food. I know it is extremely hard to get enough calories when there is not enough money to buy the right kinds of food.

Because of the high incidence of sarcoptosis, or mange, among many poor people in La Paz, I checked Constancia for blistering of the skin and itching. I am glad to report that she does not have this disease.

(continued)

Comparing Cultures

Exercise 6

Report from a Health Center Doctor

(continued)

One other thing concerns me that I must include. The Garcia family still uses many medicinal herbs to treat their illnesses. They don't get them from the witch market in La Paz, but appear to buy them from friends. There are so many people selling roots, herbs, and candies—all supposed to contain special powers to ward off spells or bring good fortune—that they are easy to obtain. Some items appear to work well, but I have real concern about others. I much prefer that they use the drugs available at our clinic.

Constancia told me other things that should be included in this report. She expressed a desire to make some money so she can buy her father a new *chullo* so his head will be protected by the warm ear flaps when he works outside. I was touched by her concern for her father and asked if her mother had a hat to wear in the market. She said yes, enthusiastically explaining that her mother's bowler hat was a gift from her sister Paulina, who is away working in Tambillo, near Lake Titicaca. Her family seems to be able to get enough clothing to keep warm.

In this section of the city we have extremely high unemployment. Her father is fortunate to get some work as a carpenter; many families have no work at all. Whatever money Constancia's parents make, however, is constantly losing value as a result of our high inflation rate. She mentioned that they seldom had money to buy all the food they needed and that they had little furniture in their home.

Constancia also talked about her younger brother Edgar. With her mother working, she must care for him much of the time. She said that Edgar gets colds so easily and then has much trouble breathing. Our high altitude does make it harder to breathe, even without a cold. I urged her to bring him to the clinic so I could examine him. She said he seems to get worse during the rainy season, which is about to begin. This is the worst time for many of our people because their homes don't protect them against the cold and damp.

Constancia told me how much she likes school, especially her classes in math and Spanish. I urged her to study her Spanish well because Aymara Indian students have a much better chance of getting work later if they know Spanish. She said she wants to work in La Paz when she is older. She promised that she would study hard.

Dr. Alfredo Murillo

Activity 4. French Fishing Family

Introduction

Louisbourg was a busy French fortress town on Cape Breton Island (formerly named Isle Royale) in Nova Scotia, Canada, during the 1740's. Many ships visited its protected harbor, bringing goods from several parts of the world and thus reducing its cultural isolation. Because of its strategic location, Louisbourg was the object of British threats, and its inhabitants constantly needed to remain vigilant against possible attack.

The fishing family described in this unit lived outside the walls of the town and in many ways was cut off from some of the products and culture of Louisbourg. Nevertheless, this family's perspective and values give us a good understanding of what it was like to live in this isolated location.

Objectives

1. To have students discover and record the major features of the culture extant in Louisbourg, Isle Royale, in the early 1740's

2. To develop students' ability to identify in another culture examples of customs, values, traditions, and technology

Time to complete

A minimum of three class sessions, with more sessions required to complete some of the supplemental assignments

---

Materials

- Present-day map of Nova Scotia, Canada
- Exercise 7: Map of Isle Royale

(continued)

Materials (continued)

- Exercise 8: History of Louisbourg
- Exercise 9: French Fishing Family
- Exercise 10: Letter from Georges de Rouches to His Brother René in Grand Pré
- Exercise 11: Report of the Gouverneur to the Minister of the Navy

Procedure

1. Locate Louisbourg on the Map of Isle Royale (Exercise 7). Next, using the present-day map of Nova Scotia, locate Louisbourg. Have students discover important information, such as elevation, population, weather, major physical features around Louisbourg, and the location of neighbors.

2. Pass out to the students Exercise 8: History of Louisbourg. Read it aloud or have students read it silently. Discuss how this history might affect the culture of the people living in Louisbourg. Record these ideas so they can be referred to later.

3. Give to each student Exercise 9: French Fishing Family—Cultural Features.

4. Ask the students to work in cooperative learning groups to locate Grand Pré and label it on the present-day map. Then have the group read Exercise 10: Letter from Georges de Rouches to His Brother René in Grand Pré. They should use information from the letter to fill in on Exercise 9 as many features as they can. After about 10 minutes, have them share aloud some of their entries for each feature. Have them finish up the work as a cooperative learning group.

5. Read aloud Exercise 11: Report of the Gouverneur to the Minister of the Navy. Then have each person add some new features to Exercise 9. Ask individuals to share items with the class, while each person writes down new items. Continue in this fashion until all information has been recorded.

6. Select six features from Exercise 9 and write them on the blackboard. Ask the students to copy these features on the back of Exercise 9. Students should form pairs and work to classify each feature as an example of custom, tradition, value, or technology. When they have completed this task, have students give their answers for each identified feature. Discuss their answers, recognizing that several terms could be used for each feature and that your task is to help students describe why they chose to classify a feature in a particular way.

Suggestions for Further Study of the French Fishing Family

- Have students read Henry Wadsworth Longfellow's poem *Evangeline*. Suggest that the students respond to the poem by writing a diary of a person who was sent out of Acadia by the British.

- Have students write to request information about the Acadians from the

  Nova Scotia Museum
  1747 Summer Street
  Halifax, Nova Scotia, B3H 3A6

  With the information obtained, create an advertising campaign designed to get more people to come from France to Louisbourg of the 1740's.

- Ask each cooperative learning group to research an aspect of life in Acadia in the 1740's and make an oral report to the whole class. Topics could include fishing practices, hunting, weapons, farming in the salt marshes, making clothing, and the use of ships for trade.

Additional Information

Fortress of Louisbourg National Historic Park
P.O. Box 160
Louisbourg, Nova Scotia
BOA 1MO

Parks Canada
Historic Properties
Upper Water Street
Halifax, Nova Scotia
B3J 1S9
(Material on Grand Pré, Port Royal,
and Fort Anne National Historic Parks)

Bibliography

Balcom, B.A. "Louisbourg." *American History* 30 (July 1995).

Bond, Nancy. *Another Shore.* New York: Macmillan Publishing Company, 1988. (Children's literature)

Daigle, John. *The Acadians of the Maritimes.* Moncton, New Brunswick: Centre d'études acadiennes, 1982.

Davidson, Marion, and Audrey Marsh. *Smoke over Grand Pré.* Halifax, Nova Scotia: Breakwater Maritimes, 1983. (Children's literature)

Downie, John, and Mary Alice Downie. *A Proper Acadian.* Toronto: Kids Can Press, 1980. (Children's literature)

Dunton, Hope. *From the Hearth: Recipes from the World of 18th Century Louisbourg.* Sydney, Nova Scotia: UCCB Press, 1986.

Fortress of Louisbourg, Coloring Book. Louisbourg: Fortress of Louisbourg Volunteers.

Fortress of Louisbourg—A Multimedia CD-ROM for Windows. Sydney, Nova Scotia: Fitzgerald Studio, 1995.

The Fortress of Louisbourg: Making History. A Video-Louisbourg. Sydney, Nova Scotia: Folkus Atlantic, 1995.

The Fortress of Louisbourg: The Grand Encampment. A Video-Louisbourg. Sydney: Folkus Atlantic, 1995.

Fraser, William. *Nor'east for Louisburg.* Toronto: Amethest Publication Limited, 1978. (Adult historical fiction)

Johnston, A.J.B. *Louisbourg, an 18th Century Town.* Halifax: Nimbus Publishing, 1991.

Krause, Eric, Carol Corbin, and William O'Shea, eds. *Aspects of Louisbourg: Essays on the History of an Eighteenth-Century French Community in North America.* Sydney: UCCB Press, 1995.

Longfellow, Henry. *Evangeline.* 3rd ed. Manchester, NH: Editions Lafayette, 1979.

Maillet, Antoine. *Pelagie.* Toronto: Central Publishing Co., 1982. (Adult historical fiction)

McLennan, J.S. *Louisbourg from Its Foundation to Its Fall.* Halifax: The Book Room Limited, 1983.

Moore, Christopher. *Fortress of Louisbourg Guide.* Louisbourg: Fortress of Louisbourg Volunteers Association, 1981.

_____. *Louisbourg Portraits*. Toronto: Macmillan of Canada, 1982.

Reardon, Chris, and A.J.B. Johnson. *Louisbourg: The Phoenix Fortress*. Halifax: Nimbus Publishing Limited, 1990.

World Wide Web

http://fortress.uccb.ns.ca/
   (Fortress of Louisbourg)

http://fortress.uccb.ns.ca/tourism/town.html
   (Town of Louisbourg)

E-mail

Louisbourg_info@pch.gc.ca

Exercise 7

Map of Isle Royale

Canada: Louisbourg, 1745.

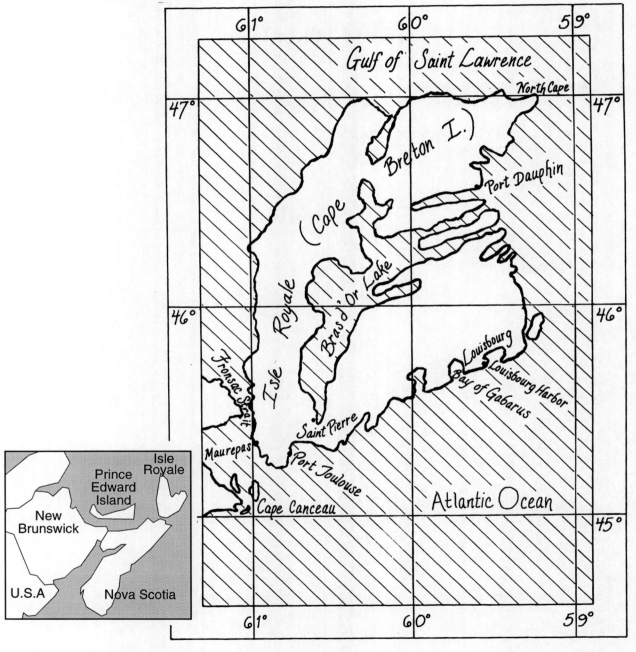

Name _____   Date _____

Exercise 8

History of Louisbourg

In April 1713, under the terms of the Treaty of Utrecht, the British took Newfoundland and Acadia from the French, allowing the French to keep only the islands in the Gulf of St. Lawrence. Among these islands was Cape Breton Island (renamed Isle Royale by the French), just north of mainland Nova Scotia.

After some initial exploring of Isle Royale, the French found a harbor on the eastern shore close to the Grand Banks, the richest fishing area in the world. This harbor would be easy to defend if a fort were built near its entrance.

In September 1713, the first settlers—116 men, 10 women, and 23 children—began the process of building homes and a fort. The settlement was named Louisbourg. The first winter was very difficult because the settlers lacked building supplies, had almost no food, and possessed very little money. These hardships made it difficult to attract new settlers, so Louisbourg grew slowly during the first few years.

Gradually, the fort took shape as more French soldiers were sent to Louisbourg. There was constant concern that the British would attack, so work continued on the fort each year. As it grew stronger, it served as a warning to England to keep away.

Despite its slow beginnings, the fortress of Louisbourg had within its walls 2,000 people by the 1740's. Many more people lived in the regions outside the walls. Louisbourg had become an important shipping port for cod, which was regularly sent to France. Ships from other parts of the world anchored in its harbor, bringing rum, molasses, sugar cane, furniture, and food.

In 1744 war broke out between Britain and France. Louisbourg was the starting point for military raids against the British towns of Canso and Annapolis Royal in Nova Scotia. The raiding was only mildly successful, so the French ships withdrew to Louisbourg. From there, soldiers tried to protect the fort against the British ships and the New England militia-men's attack in 1745. A 46-day siege resulted in Louisbourg's defeat, and by the end of the summer, its residents were all sent to France.

For four years the English held Louisbourg. Then, a truce was called, and the Treaty of Aix-la-Chapelle gave Louisbourg back to the French. By June 1749, the French settlers were back in their own homes, with the soldiers back on guard duty in the fortress. Great effort was made to strengthen the fort and to increase trade.

(continued)

Exercise 8

History of Louisbourg *(continued)*

The English were determined to remain in the area and built a large fortress and town at Halifax, several hundred miles down the coast from Louisbourg. From Halifax they, too, strengthened their positions and waited for orders. They became distrustful of the Acadians living to the west of them and finally decided to ship them entirely out of the area to other countries. A massive deportation followed, thus greatly increasing the tensions between the French and the British.

In June 1758, the British were again laying siege to Louisbourg. The superior British sea power, combined with an effective land siege, led to the fall of Louisbourg in late July. Its people were again put on ships and sent back to France.

In 1759 Louisbourg was the base for the British attempt, under the command of General Wolf, to capture Quebec. Fearing that Louisbourg would be given to France at a later date, the British completely tore down the city and the fortress in 1760. When the French signed the Treaty of Paris in 1763, they lost all claim to the land that once made up New France.

The town outside the fortress and around the harbor continued to exist, and fishing continued. In 1928 Louisbourg was recognized as a National Historic Site, and soon a museum was built. Archaeological work began, and plans were made to completely rebuild the fortress town. This rebuilding began in 1961 and continues to the present day. Tourists visiting this reconstruction, which is called the Fortress of Louisbourg National Historic Park, are able to see Louisbourg as it looked in the year 1744, when it was an important French fortress.

Home with garden in Isle Royale

Exercise 9

French Fishing Family—Cultural Features

Food	Rules and Penalties
Clothing	Type of Government
Housing	Transportation
Language	Education
Religion	Other Special Features

Exercise 10

Letter from Georges de Rouches to His
Brother René in Grand Pré

Louisbourg, Isle Royale

September 10, 1742

Dear René,

I have taken this letter to the school of the Sisters of Notre Dame so that they will put my thoughts into the best French. My lack of schooling doesn't help me write clearly what I am thinking. I envy the families that can afford to send their daughters to the Sisters' school. Even more do I envy the families who send their children back to France for schooling. But a poor fisherman can't possibly do that.

We have been catching fewer cod lately so I don't spend as much time splitting and salting the fish as I used to. We cure the cod here the same way we did in Grand Pré. I set the split cod on the wooden drying racks, then sprinkle salt all over them and let the sun do the rest. We haven't had many sunny days, however, so often I have to soak the fish in salt brine in our large barrels. As you know, that is more expensive, and I don't think the cod tastes as good either.

Fewer cod means less money for our family, but it also makes our trading here more difficult. The trading ships still come in from the West Indies with their rum, tobacco, and sugar, but we have to pay more money for them since we don't have as many cod.

Our oldest daughter, Anna, has been able to get a job as a servant in the home of one of the rich merchants. She has always been good with children, so they are having her look after their two youngest. She tells us about all the different foods and furniture they are able to import from France. She went down to the harbor with the children the other day to see newly arrived supplies from France unloaded. There was much excitement as a great crowd of people pushed up to see if the items they had ordered had arrived. We don't order much as it is so expensive. Our rough wood furniture will have to do us for quite some time yet.

Backyard gardens in Isle Royale

(continued)

Exercise 10

Letter from Georges de Rouches to His Brother René in Grand Pré *(continued)*

Things are much more prosperous here than in Grand Pré. There are many soldiers and officers around with no other place to spend their money. Our friend André has opened a tavern in a small room in his house and seems to be making a very good living. He does have to be careful not to serve the soldiers while they are on duty. He would get a very big fine and have his rum taken away.

The other day as I was walking near Frederic Gate, I saw a soldier running through the streets with an officer whipping him. I asked what he had done to deserve that and was told that he had stolen some coins from his captain. I don't imagine he will try stealing again. Soldiers are whipped quite regularly here for things they do wrong.

We are having a more difficult time getting wood for our cooking fire because so many trees have been cut near Louisbourg. There are many more people living here now, and we all want to have wood for our fires. Sometimes I have to walk a half day to get the wood. What a nuisance! I am glad I am not a hunter; they have to hunt much farther away than they did before. Even the wood for new spars and masts is now brought in from other places.

I wish you and your family would decide to move here. You must be getting tired of constantly being asked to give your support to the British. We don't have that problem here; King Louis XV seems to be doing more to make our fortress safe against British attack. Besides, we are somewhat lonely here since Gerard shipped out for France on one of the merchant vessels. He said he was tired of fishing all the time for so little pay and with only the fort for excitement. He will surely get his excitement if his ship runs into the British frigates. There seem to be more of them about lately. I can't help but worry about him.

I am having one of our traders take this letter to Fort Beausejour near you, where I trust Father La Roche will get it to you as he makes his rounds of the churches.

I will eagerly await your reply.

Your faithful brother,

Georges

Exercise 11

Report of the Gouverneur to the Minister of the Navy

Louisbourg, Isle Royale

August 18, 1742

Sire,

I wish to describe some of our problems in Louisbourg in the hope that swift action will be taken by you and King Louis XV.

We continue to be extremely short of both soldiers and military supplies. We need at least fifteen hundred muskets so that the inhabitants can be armed in case we are attacked by the British. Our gunpowder is barely adequate, and we need more of the new twelve-pound guns. We must have more money to get supplies for adding height to the royal battery to prevent it from being overrun in an attack. The housing for the troops in the barracks is very drafty because of the cracks in the stones, the lack of mortar, and the rotting wooden beams. Our soldiers complain all the time of being cold. The wooden houses of the townspeople are understandably more comfortable, but even the log walls and sod roof of the fishing family de Rouches is tighter than those drafty barracks.

We continue to have the problem of soldiers being drunk on duty. We have forbidden merchants to sell rum to soldiers on duty and on occasion have fined offenders 100 livres and taken their liquor supply. Nonetheless, this problem continues to concern us since the drunkenness often leads to criminal acts. It has gotten so bad that we have had to bring in someone from the West Indies to operate the rack for criminals.

It has been a long time since our officers have been able to return to France. Last year they agreed to stay on here even after their tour of duty was up, but we would hope that you could spare some new officers to send to us. Those who are here have been most effective with the soldiers under them. The constant sickness and near starvation have made it very hard for all of us. Anything you can do to help will be greatly appreciated.

An officer's kitchen

(continued)

         Comparing Cultures

Name _____   Date _____

Exercise 11

Report of the Gouverneur to the
Minister of the Navy *(continued)*

I would also urge you to do all you can to get new settlers for Louisbourg. We are in need of merchants who can help with the large number of trading ships that come into our harbor. Sometimes there are nearly one hundred ships tied up in our harbor at once.

I thank you for your continued efforts to make sure that the supply ships arrive at Louisbourg. Many of our merchants are quite low on silks, velvets, and linens and are being hounded by the ladies, who want to outfit their children in the latest fashions from France. Of course, there is still much cotton material around here that can be remade and patched over. Our servants are very clever at being able to make their clothing last a long time.

The newly arrived fabrics for our soldiers' breeches, vests, and greatcoats are most welcome. Many of our citizens are extremely skilled at making fine clothes from fabrics that are sent to us. We do wish there were greater opportunity to make clothing from local materials.

The last item of concern is the most serious of all. We are terribly short of food. There seems to be a poor crop of wheat in Acadia, and our ships have returned from the lands along the St. Lawrence River with little flour and few dried vegetables. We urge you to allow us to trade with New England in order to get flour and other foods from them. We have plenty of room in our storehouses and could buy and store considerably more supplies than we need immediately.

Most people have a small garden behind their houses, but we are able to grow only lettuce, carrots, spinach, and some other vegetables that do not keep through the winter. The salt pork and dark bread we have available for the soldiers during the winter gets tiresome after several months.

I must close this letter now; our Superior Council is due to hear the appeal of a merchant who thinks he was not given a fair price for window glass he imported from France.

Signed,

Gouverneur Dequesnal

Activity 5. Sasha's Family

Introduction

Sasha's family lives in St. Petersburg, a city in the Russian Federation, in the present day. Their federation is one of eleven federations that in 1991 formed the Commonwealth of Independent States out of the old Union of Soviet Socialist Republics (U.S.S.R.). Their city was founded as St. Petersburg by Czar Peter the Great, named Petrograd in 1914, Leningrad in 1924, and renamed St. Petersburg in 1991. It has played a vital role in the development of Russia and today is a major center of culture, education, and economic development.

Pavel, a cousin of Sasha, lives in Telavi, Georgia. The republic of Georgia is also a member of the Commonwealth of Independent States and a former member of the U.S.S.R. Pavel's family sent him to visit Sasha's family in St. Petersburg, thinking that soon he would have to work during his school vacations and not be able to visit his cousins and Aunt and Uncle.

Objectives

1. To have students discover and record the major features of the cultures of present-day St. Petersburg and Telavi

2. To develop students' ability to identify in another culture examples of traditions, customs, values, and technology

Time to complete

A minimum of three class periods

Materials

- Exercise 12: Map of Russia and Georgia
- Exercise 13: Sasha's Family—Cultural Features
- Exercise 14: Letter to Pavel's Family
- Exercise 15: Letter from Sasha to Pavel

Procedure

1. Using a contemporary map of the world, have students locate St. Petersburg in Russia. Encourage them to identify the members of the Commonwealth of Independent States and to compare the Commonwealth with their own country for size, longitude, latitude, and any other natural and political features they choose. Have them add key features to their copies of the map in Exercise 12.

2. Working with the class as a whole, have students tell some things they already know about Russia. If the facts are accurate, have students write these on Exercise 13: Sasha's Family—Cultural Features.

3. Have students work in small groups to read Exercise 14: Letter to Pavel's Family. As they come to specific features of the culture, have them record these features on Exercise 13.

4. Returning to the map, have students locate Telavi in the country of Georgia. Have them compare St. Petersburg and Telavi and predict some ways in which people in Telavi would have a different life from those living in St. Petersburg. Write these predictions on the blackboard, overhead, or newsprint and save them for later.

5. Give the cooperative learning groups Exercise 15: Letter from Sasha to Pavel. Have them read the letter and add more information to Exercise 13. When this is completed, have them check the accuracy of some of their guesses regarding differences in life in St. Petersburg and Telavi.

6. Ask each group of students to use library resources to prepare a short report on one of the following: history of St. Petersburg, breakup of the U.S.S.R., religious practices, communism, ethnic groups in the former U.S.S.R., Siberia, and technological and scientific achievements. Have each group read their reports as if they were a special feature on the evening news.

Suggestions for Further Study of the Russian Federation and the Republic of Georgia

- Select and read aloud several folktales from Russia and other states in the former U.S.S.R. Books of folktales are listed in the bibliography at the end of this section. Students may also enjoy reading other folktales themselves.

- Create a play about a visit to the United States by Sasha's family. Variations on that play could include a visit of the students' families or class to St. Petersburg or Telavi.

- Invite to your class someone who has lived in or visited Georgia or Russia.

- Samantha Smith was a fifth-grade student from Manchester, Maine, who wrote to Soviet premier Yuri Andropov in 1982 urging him to do more to reduce the threat of nuclear war. He wrote her a letter inviting her to come with her father and mother to visit the U.S.S.R. Their visit to the U.S.S.R. in the summer of 1983 generated much interest. The world was saddened to learn of Samantha's death in a plane crash several years later. In the summer of 1986 the Soviet government invited a group of her schoolmates to tour the U.S.S.R. Have several students read the book *Journey to the Soviet Union,* by Samantha Smith (see Bibliography), and tell the story of Samantha Smith to the class.

Resource Information on St. Petersburg, the Russian Federation, the Republic of Georgia, and the Commonwealth of Independent States

- St. Petersburg was founded in 1703 by Czar Peter the Great. It was the capital of Russia from 1712 to 1918. It is located on the delta of the Neva River, which flows into the Gulf of Finland. Landfill has connected many of the islands, but there remain numerous canals and bridges. Severe flooding occurs in the spring as the ice breaks up. The city is located almost 60 degrees north latitude and 30 degrees east longitude.

- St. Petersburg has a population of about 4.8 million people. It is a manufacturing center and the largest port in the Commonwealth of Independent States. Imports include metal pipes, factory equipment, chemicals, cotton, sugar, and fruit. Exports include machinery, timber, coal, potassium salts, and pyrites. Many people work in factories.

- The city is a major cultural center with many universities, museums, concert halls, theaters, and old churches.

- The Russian Federation, with 148 million people, consists of 21 republics, 6 territories, 49 provinces (Oblasts), 10 autonomous areas, and 2 federal cities. Its president is elected for a 5-year term. The Federal Assembly consists of 176 deputies in the Council of the Federation and 450 deputies in the State Duma. It has a Constitutional Court of 19 members.

- The Commonwealth of Independent States is a confederation of independent states formerly among the constituent republics of the Soviet Union. It was established in 1991, following a summit in the Belarusian city of Brest, at which the U.S.S.R. was dissolved. The 11 member states sited the administrative headquarters in the Belarusian city of Minsk. It is not referred to much in news stories and seems to have very little involvement in the day-to-day running of its constituent states.

- Surrounded by Russia, Turkey, Armenia, and Azerbaijan, the Republic of Georgia has a population of 5.43 million people. It became an independent state in April 1991, and Eduard Shevardnadze assumed leadership in 1992. He implemented democratic and market-oriented reforms, and Georgia joined the Commonwealth of Independent States and the United Nations. After considerable internal struggle, Georgia approved a new constitution in 1995, and Shevardnadze was elected to a 5-year term as president. Parliament has 246 seats. Georgia is a presidental republic with federal elements. It grows grain, tea, potatoes, vegetables, berries, fruit, and especially grapes used to make wine and brandy.

Bibliography

Afanas'ev, Alexander. *Russian Folktales.* New York: Pantheon, 1975.

Amery, Heather, and Katrina Kirilenko. *The First Thousand Words in Russian.* London: Osborne Publishing Co., 1983. (Children's literature)

Dabars, Zita. *The Russian Way.* Lincolnwood, IL: Passport Books, 1997.

Deltenre, Chantal, and Martine Noblet. *Tintin's Travel Diaries: Russia.* Hauppauge, NY: Barron's Educational Series, Inc., 1995. (Children's literature)

Gachechiladze, Revaz. *The New Georgia: Space, Society, Politics.* College Station, TX: Texas A & M Press, 1995.

Goldenberg, Suzanne. *Pride of Small Nations: The Caucasus and Post-Soviet Disorder.* New York: Zed Books, Ltd., 1994.

Jacobsen, Peter. *A Family in the U.S.S.R.* New York: Bookwright Press, 1988. (Children's literature)

Kimmel, Eric. *Baba Yaga.* New York: Holiday House, 1991. (Children's literature)

Lapenkova, Valentina. *Russian Food and Drink.* New York: Bookwright Press, 1988. (Children's literature)

Laskey, Katherine. *The Night Journey.* New York: Viking Penguin, 1981. (Children's literature)

Lerner Publishers, ed. *The Soviet Union in Pictures.* Minneapolis: Lerner Publishers, 1989. (Children's literature)

Massie, Susan. *Land of the Firebird: The Beauty of Old Russia.* New York: Simon and Schuster, 1980.

Matlock, David, and Valerie Matlock. *Russian Walks.* New York: Henry Holt and Co., 1991.

Neville, Peter. *A Traveler's History of Russia and the USSR.* New York: Interlink Books, 1997.

Noble, John, et. al. *Russia, Ukraine & Belarus.* Oakland, CA: Lonely Planet Publications, 1996.

Pushkin, Alexander. *The Tale of the Dead Princess and the Seven Knights.* Moscow: Progress Publishers, 1973. (Children's literature)

Ransome, Arthur. *Old Peter's Russian Tales.* New York: Viking Penguin, 1985. (Children's literature)

Raymer, Steve. "St. Petersburg: Capital of the Tzars." *National Geographic,* Vol. 184 (December 1993), pp. 96–121.

_____. *St. Petersburg.* Atlanta: Turner Publishing Company, 1994.

Richards, Susan. *Epics of Everyday Life.* New York: Viking Penguin, 1990.

Richardson, Dan, and Rob Humphreys. *St. Petersburg: The Rough Guide.* 2d ed. London: The Rough Guides, Ltd., 1995.

Salisbury, Harrison. *The 900 Days: The Siege of Leningrad.* New York: Harper and Row, 1969.

Smith, Anne Galicich. *Samantha Smith: A Journey for Peace.* Minneapolis: Dillon Press, 1987.

Smith, Hedrick. *The New Russians.* New York: Random House, 1990.

Smith, Samantha. *Journey to the Soviet Union.* Boston: Little Brown, 1985. (Children's literature)

Stanley, Diane. *Peter the Great.* New York: Four Winds Press, 1986. (Children's literature)

Suny, Ronald. *The Making of the Georgian Nation.* 2d ed. Bloomington: Indiana University Press, 1994.

Warner, Elizabeth. *Heroes, Monsters and Other Worlds from Russian Mythology.* New York: Schocken Books, 1985. (Children's literature)

Yolen, Jane. *Favorite Folktales from Around the World.* New York: Pantheon, 1985.

Zheleznikov, Vladimir. *Scarecrow.* New York: Harper Collins, 1990. (Children's literature)

World Wide Web

http://www.russiatoday.com
(Connections to many sites from this one site)

Name _____   Date _____

Exercise 12

Map of Russia and Georgia

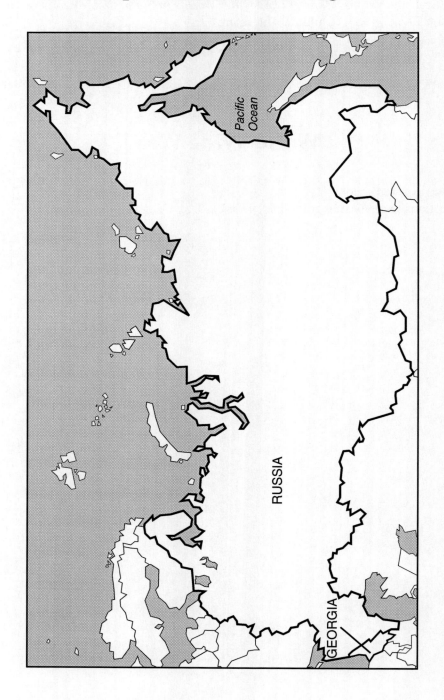

Comparing Cultures

Exercise 13

Sasha's Family—Cultural Features

Food	Rules and Penalties
Clothing	Type of Government
Housing	Transportation
Language	Education
Religion	Other Special Features

Exercise 14

Letter to Pavel's Family

St. Petersburg, Russia

July

Dear Family,

I have been here nearly two weeks and Sasha and Uncle Aleksandr and Aunt Galina have kept me busy. I still think a lot about you and wonder how you are doing. We get some news about the Georgian Republic, but I don't see our home city Telavi mentioned at all. It seemed so large and important when I was living there. Tell my friends I say hello.

Living in a huge concrete-block apartment building is so different from our house. There are more than a thousand people in our building, and there are about 20 buildings just like ours nearby. I still am not used to so many people in one small area. St. Petersburg still has a housing shortage, a result of the 900-day siege during the Second World War. Much of the housing was destroyed, and they have not been able to build enough to house everybody. Sasha says that he had to learn all about that siege in school. That was something I didn't read much about, since we studied more about the history of the Georgian Republic during the Second World War.

We always take the elevator to the tenth floor, although I sometimes wonder if the elevator will make it. Sasha likes taking it because the stairs are always so dark and drafty. The apartment is small, so I have to sleep in his room. Cousin Yuliya lives here too, although I don't see much of her. She has a boyfriend, and they go out a lot.

What I miss most here are our persimmon trees, grapevines over our patio, and chickens in the yard. But it is not as hot here as it is in Telavi, so I don't need the shade as much. I still can't get used to the fact that we have to buy everything we eat at a store. Aunt Galina cooks many things I like, but we don't have as much variety here as we have at home. Getting beef is the hardest. There just doesn't seem to be any available. There are always turnips and cabbages. Occasionally we are able to have sausage.

Homes and church at Telavi

(continued)

Exercise 14

Letter to Pavel's Family *(continued)*

Yesterday I was telling Sasha about the dance group I belong to. I showed him how I could hit my boot with my hand as I did one of our fancy steps. He tried to do it and fell down. I told him it took lots of practice before I was able to do that step. He thought that he would like to have the bright red tunics and black belt and boots I wear. I wish I could have the dance troupe here to show him how good we are.

Last week we all took the Metro (subway) downtown. I was surprised at how fast the train went and how bright and richly decorated the stations were. We came out of the subway near the Admiralty and walked along Nevsky Prospect to the State Hermitage Museum. It is so huge we only went to the Winter Palace, which was the winter home of the imperial family. Uncle Aleksandr had been there many times, so he took us to some things he thought we would like to see. I liked the Malachite Hall the best. Almost everything there is made of green stone with black swirls. I had never seen anything so rich before. I can see why the imperial family gathered there for ceremonies. Sasha and I got so tired that we left, even though Uncle Aleksandr said we had not seen even a small part of what was in the museum.

When we got on to Nevsky Prospect, we walked along looking in many store windows. There are more things to buy here than we have at home. I even saw some blue jeans and a sweater in one store window. Sasha told me that I had just missed being able to go to the movies with him. He said he walks along Nevsky Prospect at 1:00 in the morning and it is as bright as daylight. Aunt Galina said that it is like a giant party with many people all walking and talking. I think that would be so much fun to do. He said it is so light in June because they are so much farther north than we are. I managed to find things I was able to buy. Some of them are gifts for you all so I am not going to tell you what I got. Here we buy things that are available in the stores because we never know when they will be available again.

(continued)

Exercise 14

Letter to Pavel's Family *(continued)*

Sasha and I play soccer with his friends. I am just as good as the others, and our games are exciting. I am going to need to buy a new pair of shoes if I play much more, though. Sasha says we can get a pair at a store near the apartment. Some of his friends have shoes that are imported, but Sasha's are made in Russia.

I have so much to tell you when I see you. We have lots more things planned to do. Everybody here says to give you greetings, especially Uncle Aleksandr, who says he misses Georgia a great deal. He has told me a lot about growing up in Tbilisi.

Love,

Pavel

School group dance—Tbilisi

Exercise 15

Letter from Sasha to Pavel

St. Petersburg, Russia

November

Dear Pavel,

It seems like so long ago that you were here with us. As you know, I have gotten myself heavily involved in after-school activities, so I haven't much time left for writing letters. My clarinet lessons are going well. Earlier this month I was able to play in a concert at the Palace of Youth with a youth orchestra. Several in my school are in the orchestra.

Our good news is that my sister Yuliya is going to be married to Anton in the spring. As I recall, you liked him a lot when you were here with us. They will go to the Palace of Weddings for the ceremony; then we will have a party at our apartment for our families and friends. My mother is already planning the menu. Several of her friends have offered to help, too. I wish we could have that cheese-filled bread (I think you called it *khachapuri)* that your mother sent along with you when you came to visit us. We can't get that anywhere in St. Petersburg. My mother does make delicious sweet rolls and cakes, though, and I like all the herring, meat dumplings, smoked salmon, eel, and pickled mushrooms we will have. Father's salary from teaching has been reduced again, so we won't be able to have caviar.

Yuliya and Anton will need to live in our apartment, since there is no housing available for them right now. That will make it much more crowded, but I like Anton. He is studying about computers at St. Petersburg State University, so that he can work with a bank. My parents say that Yuliya and Anton may be able to find housing in about three years.

This year the courses I like the most are geography, literature, and math. My exams are in May, so I am studying hard to pass them. Yuliya says that in order to be able to go to the university, I will have to do better on my tests. I am not sure what I will study there. For a while I was interested in being in government, but now with all the changes, I don't see that as very appealing. Perhaps I will study computers too, like Anton.

As you recall from your summer visit, our food is hard to get and expensive. We can still buy cabbage and beets in the stores, and I look forward to the good *borscht* that mother makes with the cabbage and beets. I don't imagine you are having the same problems with food there, as it is grown on the farms all around Telavi. Our major concern now is whether we will have enough heat for the winter.

(continued)

Exercise 13

Letter from Sasha to Pavel *(continued)*

Our city government is having trouble paying the electrical workers and has to loan the electric company money to buy oil for making electricity.

I watch our newspapers for stories about Georgia. Yesterday I read a story about President Shevardnadze and how he is trying to encourage more tourists to come to the Republic of Georgia. From the pictures you showed me when you were here, there would be many places in your town that would interest tourists. I liked seeing how different your houses looked from what we have in St. Petersburg.

Would you like me to get you a record of the latest rock music being played around St. Petersburg? I was in Grammplastinki the other day and found several really good records that I think you would like. Remember how much my parents complained about how loud we played the CD's? They still do, but I like it loud so I can feel the beat. I wonder what they listened to when they were growing up.

How has the harvest gone for your parents' cooperative? Earlier you wrote that it looked as though the grapes would be very good this year. My mother wants to see if she can find some of the wine made in your area of Georgia for Yuliya's wedding. It would be fun to imagine that your parents picked the grapes that made the wine. My father says that Georgian wine is the best he has tasted.

Catherine's Palace

At the end of our study of our great poet Aleksandr Pushkin, our literature class at school took a train to the town where he was born in 1799. We got to look at the museum in the Lycee, the school where Pushkin went when he was young. We also went through the museum, where many pages of his manuscript are on display. I saw in the nearby park the statue of the "Girl with a Pitcher" that he wrote about. The trip made his writing come alive for me. I can see why later his hometown was named for him.

We also went through some of the buildings that were used by the royal family when Pushkin was growing up. Most of the buildings were destroyed during World War II but are restored now.

Let me hear from you.

Your cousin,

Sasha

Activity 6. Seoul Family

Introduction

The Republic of Korea has a long history of occupation by foreign powers. Despite this occupation, a distinctive Korean culture exists with roots more than 2,000 years old. Hosting the 1988 Summer Olympics helped introduce Korean vitality to people in other parts of the world. However, the complexity of such an ancient culture is impossible to capture in snap-shots—either of the Olympics or in this brief presentation. Recently, political corruption and economic difficulties have left the Korean Republic more reliant on aid from the United States, many other nations, and the World Bank.

Objectives

1. To have students discover and record the major features and history of the culture of the Republic of Korea

2. To develop students' ability to identify in another culture examples of customs, traditions, values, and technology

Time to complete

A minimum of three class sessions, with more time required if supplemental activities are undertaken

---

Materials

- Exercise 16: Map of Korea
- Exercise 17: Seoul Family—Cultural Features
- Exercise 18: History of Korea
- Exercise 19: Letter to Grandparents in Kongju
- Exercise 20: School Report on Korean Traditions

Procedure

1. Use the class map of Korea to identify the following: Korea's neighbors; the 38th parallel, with the demilitarized zone dividing North and South Korea; Seoul; Kongju; and bodies of water surrounding Korea. Ask the students to add this information to their map in Exercise 16. Have them use what they already know to make predictions about Korea's history and economic situation. They should write down their predictions and save them for later use.

2. Read to the students Exercise 17: History of Korea. Compare their predictions with the actual history, focusing on the clues from the map that helped them make their predictions.

3. Distribute to the students Exercise 18: Seoul Family—Cultural Features. Then ask each group to read together Exercise 19: Letter to Grandparents in Kongju. When they have finished, have them write the appropriate information on the Seoul Family activity. Use the same procedure with Exercise 20: School Report.

4. Ask each student to write a one-paragraph statement explaining why he or she would choose to live in either Kongju or Seoul. Have them share these statements with their groups.

5. Assign to each group one of the cultural features not adequately covered in the material on the exercises. Each group should give a brief presentation to the whole class sharing the information they have found. Students should write this information on Exercise 18.

6. Divide the class in half. Have one group work on the activity suggested in (a) and the other half work on the activity suggested in (b) below. When the pairs from each half are through, form teams of four by putting together one pair from (a) and one pair from (b). Have them present their ideas to each other.

   (a) Compose a list of reasons why the Republic of Korea might have wanted to host the 1988 Summer Olympic Games. Compose a list of reasons that might have been given for not hosting the Summer Olympics.

   (b) Compose a list of reasons why South Korea might want to unite with North Korea. Compose a list of reasons that South Korea might give for not uniting with North Korea.

Suggestions for Further Study of the Republic of Korea

• Have students find in magazines and books pictures of statues of the Buddha. Ask them to draw a statue themselves and include on their drawing a paragraph explaining who the Buddha was and giving some details about his teaching.

• Read aloud to the class a Korean folktale. (Several books are listed in the bibliography of this section.) Have the students perform a dramatic recreation of one of the tales. *Blindman's Daughter* and *Two Brothers and Their Magic Gourd* would be appropriate. Both are edited by Edward B. Adams. They can be purchased from

Arthur M. Sackler Gallery Gift Shop
1050 Independence Avenue, S.W.
Washington, D.C. 20560

• Invite to your classroom people who have visited or lived in the Republic of Korea. Ask each student to write down one question for the visitor. Conduct a class interview with the visitor, and have each student record the visitor's answer to his or her question.

• Ask students to write a short story in which their home country is taken over by a foreign power. Tell them to use the experience of the people in the Republic of Korea as a model for writing their story. If there is time, have them read their stories aloud. If there is not time, display the stories for others to read.

• Many areas of the Korean Republic have Western food chains, like McDonald's, Burger King, Pizza Hut, and KFC, with many more chains planning to open soon. There are also many Western clothing stores, including DKNY, Benetton, Levis, and Reebok. Conduct a discussion of the following two questions:
 (1) What might happen to Korean culture if half of the stores in large cities are not of Korean origin?
 (2) If young people wear clothes and eat food that is generally recognized as Western, what makes them Korean?

Resource Information About the Republic of Korea

• The Korean peninsula is about 600 miles long and 135 miles wide. The southern 45 percent of the peninsula is the Republic of Korea (South Korea). The Democratic People's Republic of Korea (North Korea) occupies the rest of the peninsula. About 80 percent of the land is mountains and hills. The country has cold winters. Humid summers include a monsoon season that brings half of the rain that falls during the year. There are occasional typhoons in late summer and cyclones in late spring. Numerous rivers, most of which flow into the Yellow Sea, provide water for irrigation of the important rice crop.

- The population is homogeneously Korean. The national language is Korean, and the writing system, *Han'gul*, contains ten vowels and fourteen consonants. Words from the Chinese language make up more than one half of the vocabulary. There are about 46 million people living in the Republic of Korea, with Seoul having about 10 million people. About one third of the population is younger than 15 years old. Small family farms employ one third of the population.

- The country is currently operating under the constitution of the Sixth Republic, which began in February 1988 when Roh Tae-Woo was elected president. It provides for a highly centralized presidential system of government. The president serves one five-year term. A prime minister is appointed by the president. There are 299 members of the National Assembly, and they serve four-year terms. At age 20 all citizens can vote. The Supreme Court chief justice is appointed by the president with the approval of the National Assembly. All other justices are appointed by the president.

- Religious beliefs include shamanism (spirits reside in inanimate objects), Confucianism, Buddhism, and Christianity.

- Six years of primary education is compulsory and free. Almost all children attend primary schools. Three fourths attend three-year middle schools and three-year general or vocational high schools. Getting into the right university is very important, and students work extremely hard all during high school to prepare for the entrance exam. How they do on the exam will determine whether they will be able to go on to a university, and which ones will accept them. There is a national literacy rate of 95 percent.

Bibliography

Adams, Edward B. *Korea's Golden Age: Cultural Spirit of Silla in Kyongju.* Seoul: Seoul International Publishing House, 1991.

———. ed. *Blindman's Daughter.* Seoul: Seoul International Publishing House, 1981. (All books by Adams are children's literature)

———. *Herdboy and Weaver.* Seoul: Seoul International Publishing House, 1981.

———. *Two Brothers and Their Magic Gourd.* Seoul: Seoul International Publishing House, 1982.

———. *Woodcutter and Nymph.* Seoul: Seoul International Publishing House, 1982.

Ashby, Gwynneth. *A Family in South Korea*. Minneapolis: Lerner Publications, 1987. (Children's literature)

Belgassi, Haemi. *Peacebound Trains*. Boston: Clarion Books, 1996. (Children's literature)

Choi, Sook Myul. *Echoes of the White Giraffe*. Boston: Houghton Mifflin, 1993. (Children's literature)

_____. *Year of the Impossible Goodbyes*. Boston: Houghton Mifflin Co., 1996. (Children's literature)

Chung, Kyung, Phyllis Haffner, and Fredric Kaplan. *The Korea Guidebook*. Boston: Houghton Mifflin Co., 1991.

Climo, Shirley. *The Korean Cinderella*. New York: Harper Collins, 1993. (Children's literature)

Covell, Jon. *Korea's Cultural Roots*. Elizabeth, NJ: Hollym International, 1982. (Children's literature)

Gibbons, Boyd. "The South Koreans." *National Geographic,* Vol. 174 (August 1988), pp. 232–257.

Jacobson, Karen. *Korea*. Chicago: Children's Press, 1989. (Children's literature)

Kearney, Robert. *The Warrior Worker: The Challenge of the Korean Way of Working*. New York: Henry Holt and Co., 1991.

Kraus, Joanna. *Tall Boy's Journey*. Minneapolis: Carolrhoda Books, 1992.

Lee, Marie. *Saying Goodbye*. Boston: Houghton Mifflin, 1993. (Children's literature)

Leeke, Ada. *When Americans Came to Korea*. Freeman, SD: Pine Hill Press, 1991.

McGowan, Tom. *The Korean War*. New York: Franklin Watts, 1992. (Children's literature)

McMahon, Patricia. *Chi-hoon: A Korean Girl*. Honesdale, PA: Boyds Mills Press, 1993. (Children's literature)

Moffett, Eileen F. *Korean Ways*. Seoul: Seoul International Publishing House, 1986.

Nahm, Andrew. *A Panorama of 5000 Years: Korean History*. Elizabeth, NJ: Hollym International, 1983. (Children's literature)

Newman, Kathy. "Kyongju, Where Korea Began." *National Geographic,* Vol. 174 (August 1988).

Nilson, Robert. *South Korea Handbook*. 2d ed. Chico, CA: Moon Publications, 1997.

Solberg, S.E. *The Land and People of Korea.* New York: Harper Collins, 1991. (Children's literature)

Stein, R. Conrad. *The Korean War: The Forgotten War.* Hillside, NJ: Enslow Publishers, 1994.

Tolan, Sally, Mary Lee Knowlton, and Mark Sachner, eds. *Children of the World: South Korea.* Milwaukee: Gareth Stevens Publishing, 1987. (Children's literature)

Watkins, Yoko. *So Far from the Bamboo Grove.* New York: Lothrop, Lee and Shepard, 1986. (Children's literature)

Yoo, Yushin. *Korea the Beautiful: Treasures of the Hermit Kingdom.* Murray, KY: Golden Pond, 1987. (Children's literature)

World Wide Web Sites

http://www.koreaherald.co.kr/

http://www.korea.com

Exercise 16

Map of South Korea

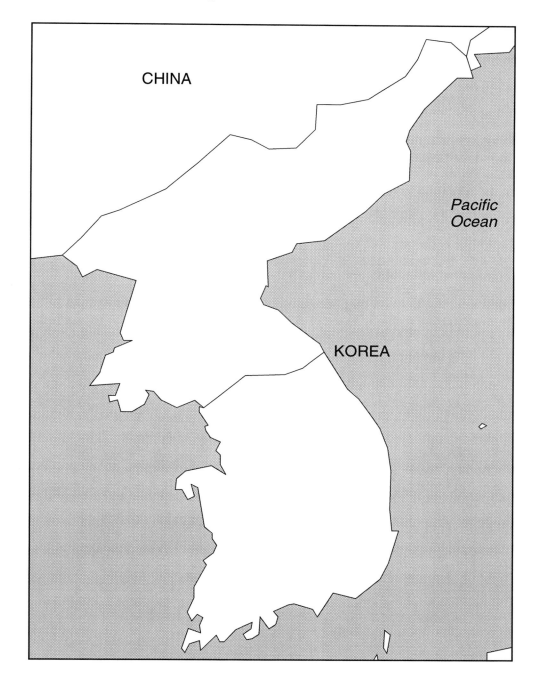

Name _____   Date _____

History of Korea

Korea is a 600-mile-long peninsula the size of Utah. Well before 300 B.C., powerful leaders called feudal lords gathered around them people who would farm their land and, when necessary, fight against other feudal lords. For many centuries fighting was a way of life for the settlers of Korea.

Over a period of seven centuries, starting around 57 B.C., small groups of people began to unite into more powerful groups. Three kingdoms emerged, and toward the end of the seventh century A.D., the Silla kingdom cooperated with the Chinese to defeat both the Paekche and the Koguryo kingdoms. Shortly afterward, Silla pushed the Chinese out and unified the Korean peninsula under its rule. What followed was a blending of Korean and Chinese customs. Buddhism became the dominant religion, but Confucianism also was very strong. Many temples were built, art was encouraged, and education became very important. During the next century the city of Kyongju became the fourth largest city in the world. The rule of the Silla continued for the next several centuries; by A.D. 935 the leader Wang Kon grew strong enough to unite the peninsula under a new state, Koryo, and to begin a dynasty that was to last for 450 years.

Continuous conflict with the Chinese weakened the power of the dynasty and led to the Mongol invasion from the north in the middle of the thirteenth century. The Mongols took large annual tributes of gold, silver, horses, and women. Nevertheless, during their occupation, the Koreans gained knowledge of astrology, medicine, cotton cultivation, and artistic skills.

After the Mongols had been driven out, there emerged a major new leader, Yi Song-gye, who resumed relations with China and established Confucianism as the dominant religion. All during its rule, the Yi dynasty had to deal with attempted invasions by Japan and strong pressure from the Manchus in China. In the 1800's, despite some financial progress, Korea experienced major social unrest. Contact with people and ideas from the West was discouraged. Japan and China continued their struggle for Korea. In 1876 Japan and Korea signed a peace treaty.

From 1910 to the end of the Second World War in 1945, the Japanese had possession of Korea. During that time, Korean ideas and language were discouraged. During the Second World War, Korean workers took jobs vacated by Japanese workers, who were required to fight.

(continued)

Exercise 17

History of Korea *(continued)*

When Japan lost the war, North and South Korea were temporarily divided, and plans for a provisional government were agreed to. The United States maintained a strong presence in the south, while the Soviet Union assumed responsibility for guiding the recovery of the north. Few Koreans supported this plan; in addition, the working relationship between the United States and the Soviet Union broke down. The United Nations became involved in trying to reunify the two Koreas. Elections were held in the south, and on August 15, 1948, 73-year-old Syngman Rhee became the first president of the Republic of Korea. The north became the Democratic People's Republic of Korea and was governed by Kim Il-song.

Civil war broke out in 1950 when troops from the north invaded the south and pushed the Republic of Korea troops almost to Pusan in the south. United Nations troops, supplied mostly by the United States, came to the aid of the Republic of Korea. Three years later, a truce was signed, and a permanent division was made at the 38th parallel. Both sides were devastated by the war. They have since had separate governments with no contact allowed between peoples.

Kim Il-song remained the leader in the north. Syngman Rhee continued in the south until he resigned in 1960. After an interim, General Park Chung-hee became president of the Republic of Korea in 1961. He served until his assassination in 1979. With a new constitution in 1980, the Fifth Republic began. In August 1980, the National Assembly elected General Chun to a seven-year term as president. World recognition of the economic health of the Republic of Korea came with its selection as host of the 1988 Summer Olympic Games. Just prior to that event a general election was held, and Roh Tae-Woo was elected president, marking the start of the Sixth Republic. He served as president until 1992, when Kim Young-Sam was elected as the first civilian to be president in 30 years. Talks about uniting North and South Korea continued to be held during his presidency. Bribery and bankruptcies also happened during his term in office. New elections were held in December 1997, and Kim Dae Jung was elected. He took charge in February 1998, with massive foreign debt problems.

Buddhist temple in Seoul

Exercise 18

Seoul Family—Cultural Features

Food	Rules and Penalties
Clothing	Type of Government
Housing	Transportation
Language	Education
Religion	Other Special Features

Exercise 19

Letter to Grandparents in Kongju

Seoul, Korea

July

Dear Grandfather and Grandmother,

I am helping Mother get ready for Yeo's first birthday party. I am so excited that you will be able to come. We have already made lots of rice cakes and candies. Next week I will go with Mother to the market to buy the apples, muskmelon, pears, and tangerines. I hope there are some strawberries too, because these are my favorite fruit. Yeo gets excited every time we mention her birthday *Tol*.

Mother was telling me about my first birthday *Tol*. She said you both were here. When it came time to play the game of prophecy, she told me that I touched the book and the thread but finally picked the pencil to keep for my own. Father was so excited because he thought that meant I would be a writer. I wonder what Yeo will pick. It would be good if she chooses the money. I would like to have a sister who is wealthy, so I could have things I like.

You will like the special jacket and skirt Mother has made for her. I hope you will wear your beautiful old *hanbok*, Grandmother. I like the bright colors in the skirt and the long ribbon tie on the jacket. Mother says that she doesn't see very many women wearing *hanbok* in downtown Seoul. Most of the women and men wear the kinds of suits and dresses that you see in large Western cities. I like my clothes to be mostly in the Western style. I particularly like the blue jeans I got last week.

Father took us downtown on the subway the other day. We got to play at the playground halfway up Mt. Namsan. We put Yeo in a swing and pushed her. She laughed and laughed. Then we took a bus to the top of the Seoul Tower. Father pointed out many of the gates from the old city of Seoul. I saw some of the Olympic buildings as well. Father said that he had taken me up here a long time ago, but I don't remember it. I liked looking out and seeing how huge our city is.

Street scene in Seoul

(continued)

Exercise 19

Letter to Grandparents
in Kongju *(continued)*

Will the Paekche Cultural Festival in Kongju be held in early October this year? I asked Mother if we can come visit you while that is going on, but she said Whan and I will be in school and can't afford to miss the classes. I remember the last time we were with you for the festival; I thought the street procession honoring the ancient kings would never end. The costumes worn by the court maidens and loyal subjects were decorated with such pretty silk designs. The traditional music and dancing were also interesting. The dancers moved to the music so smoothly they seemed to float.

Have more people been coming to the festival since the tomb of King Muryong and his queen was discovered? It is hard for me to imagine what life was like in A.D. 510. When you took us to the museum to see some of the relics, I remember that Whan was fascinated by all the weapons. He kept making strange noises as he pretended to charge at me with a sword. He surprised me when he said he liked the porcelain lamps, too. My favorite relic was a gold ornament in the shape of a flower.

Sometimes Yeo comes out in the garden with me when I go to gather some vegetables. I have to watch her very carefully because she doesn't know the difference between the weeds and the sesame leaves or spinach leaves or radishes. She has learned not to pull up the mung beans and the soybeans because these now have pods that are easy to see. She will put these in her mouth and eat them raw, though! I much

Vegetables in Chongju

prefer them in the soups that Mother makes with the fermented soybeans. I hope you will bring some of your special cabbage *kimchi* when you come for Yeo's birthday *Tol*. Yours is so much better than what we buy in the store here. It is delicious with rice.

I look forward to seeing you soon.

Love,

Sook Min

Exercise 20

School Report on Korean Traditions

by Yoo Whan Ho

This report describes some of the ways in which my grandparents' and their parents' lives were the same. My grandparents' home in Kongju belonged to my grandfather's parents. Very little about the house has been changed. It is located near the edge of the city on land that has a small garden plot. The house is one story, with small windows and two outside doors. An outside wooden porch is used for eating and visiting in the hot summer.

Inside the house are two rooms. The kitchen has a large cooking area where a wood fire supplies the heat for cooking. Many herbs are hung around the kitchen. My grandmother goes into the countryside to collect wild herbs for cooking. She also grows herbs in her garden. The heat from the kitchen fire—and in the winter, from another fire built near the foundation in the kitchen—is used to heat the *ondol* room in the house. The hot smoke flows through ducts under the floor of the *ondol* room and then leaves from a chimney on the other side of the room. The floor of the room stays warm as long as the fires are burning.

The *ondol* room is the main room of the house. It is used for eating and, when the dining table is put away, for sleeping as well. The floor is laid with flagstones that are covered by clay and by a heavy waxed paper that helps conduct heat into the room. Since people sit on the floor to eat and lie on thin mats to sleep, their bodies keep in contact with a warm floor. This kind of heating has been used in Korea for about two thousand years. Many of my grandparents' friends now use coal and hot water to heat the floors, but my grandfather says he would rather do things the traditional way. My grandparents have also kept the old custom of having the toilet in the backyard.

Before we enter their house, we put our shoes on a stepstone outside the door. The inside walls are lined with a specially prepared paper that serves as insulation against cold and heat. It is white, but the screens that stand in several rooms

On the way home in Chongju

have colorful designs. The house seems as if it is hundreds of years old.

(continued)

Exercise 20

School Report on Korean
Traditions (continued)

In the fall my grandparents make *kimchi*. Grandmother cuts, washes, and salts about 60 heads of cabbage, along with many white radishes. These vegetables are mixed with red peppers, garlic, and ginger; pickled; and put in thick pottery jars. The jars are then buried up to their necks in the ground. All the ingredients ferment to make a tasty food that is available all winter. During the summer they make more fancy *kimchi* by adding things like eggplant, turnip, pine nuts, salted shrimp, and oysters.

Grandfather tells me that all during the fall, while people are making their *kimchi*, they ask each other about the progress they are making on their *kimchi*. He says that the time for making *kimchi* in the fall is called *kimjang*.

Another tradition is one my family takes part in. Every lunar New Year's Day we dress in our best clothes, leave our home in Seoul, and go to Kongju to be with my grandparents. My cousins and their parents also come. The most important part of our celebration is when we children honor our grandparents. My grandparents are seated on the floor of the *ondol* room dressed in their best clothes. All of us bow low in front of them, almost touching our heads to the floor. It is a time to show them how much we respect our elders. As a way of showing appreciation for the honor, my grandparents give us some small coins, which we may use to buy toys or candy.

The younger children play games, and then we have our special meal. Grand-mother has fixed many different dishes for us: fish, barbecued beef, soups, and, of course, rice.

Sometimes we are able to stay at their home for several days, since New Year's is a national holiday. It is the only time our whole family is together, because my cousins live in the south in Taegu. When Grandfather was young, it was the tradi-tion to live in the same place as your father. This is one tradition that our family has not kept: Father is in Seoul, and his brother is in Taegu.

Activity 7. Two Tasmanian Families

Introduction

The island state of Tasmania is well known to many students as the dwelling place of the Tasmanian devil. Their interest in this animal can be the means to expand their knowledge of the country that is its host. In fact, it is the interest of two Tasmanian children in the Tasmanian devil that helps them develop a friendship using their respective schools' E-mail links. One, Robyn, is located in Hobart, the capital of Tasmania; the other, Gary, is located in New Norfolk, a small town located about 25 miles from Hobart.

Objectives

1. To have students discover and record the major features of the culture of the present-day state of Tasmania, in Australia

2. To develop students' ability to identify in another culture examples of traditions, customs, values, and technology

Time to complete

A minimum of three class sessions, with more time required if supplementary activities are undertaken

---

Materials

- Exercise 21: Map of Tasmania and Australia
- Exercise 22: Two Tasmanian Families—Cultural Features
- Exercise 23: Initial E-mail Contact
- Exercise 24: E-mail Contact a Week Later

Procedure

1. Using the map of Tasmania and Australia, Exercise 21, conduct a study of the geography of Tasmania. Locate and label Hobart, New Norfolk, Port Arthur, Brighton, and the Derwent Valley. Help students think about what it means for Tasmania to be the only island state in Australia. Define the term *the roaring 40's,* and describe how boats traveling from the tip of Africa toward Tasmania are affected by the winds.

2. Have students make a list of all the things they know about the Tasmanian devil. Then have them make a list of what they want to know. Post both lists where students can see them, so as they learn more about the Tasmanian devil, they can add that information to their class list.

3. Distribute Exercise 22: Two Tasmanian Families—Cultural Features. Then have students work in small groups to read Exercise 23: Initial E-mail Contact. As they come to specific features of the culture in Tasmania, have them record these features on Exercise 22. Tell the students that the E-mail addresses for Gary and Robyn are made up. However, the E-mail address for the University of Tasmania Zoology Department is a real World Wide Web address.

4. If your students have access to computers in your classroom or school library, have them work in small teams and log on to several of the sites suggested in the Bibliography. If you do not have access to computers in the school, some students might volunteer to make reports based on information they gathered from their home computer.

   For their reports, students can include one or more of the following ideas: things they could do if they lived in Hobart, current weather and temperature, any local news stories they find, or information about other parts of Tasmania.

5. Have students work in small groups to read Exercise 24: E-mail Contact a Week Later. As they come to specific features of the culture in Tasmania, have them record these features on Exercise 22.

6. Have half the class assume that they are Gary, living near New Norfolk, and the other half the class assume that they are Robyn, living in Hobart. Have each team construct a final E-mail letter that their person would send to the other. Exchange the E-mail letters and, as a whole class, talk about how realistic their communication sounded.

Suggestions for Further Study of Tasmania

1. People lived in Australia long before the British sent their early settlers and prisoners. These aboriginal people had a life very different from that of the British

settlers. Have teams of students study the aboriginal people in Tasmania and other parts of Australia and report to the class about their findings. Things they could focus on would be where they lived, what they ate, how they moved about the country, how they were treated by the British settlers, and the quality of their life today.

2. Starting in 1787, the British government sent prisoners to Australia. Many remained in prisons for a very long time, while some were released fairly quickly to settle in Australia. Tasmania was a major location for their prisons. Have students study the early prison system and report to the class about things like the trip from Great Britain to Australia, the prison environment, settlement, and the formation of early government in Tasmania.

3. Far in advance of studying about Tasmania, have students contact the "Aussie Helpline" and request information about Tasmania and other parts of Australia. It would help to explain that they are using the information for a study of Tasmania. In North America the best place to receive information about Australia and Tasmania in particular is the "Aussie Helpline" run by the Australian Tourist Commission at P.O. Box 7925, Mt. Prospect, IL 60056.

4. With the tourist material on Tasmania, have five teams of students do a project that includes: (1) planning the route for a one-week bus trip around Tasmania for their group; (2) deciding for each day where the class members will stay and where they will eat; (3) planning what the group will visit each day; (4) calculating approximately how much it will cost the group to go on this trip.

5. Find people in the community who have visited Tasmania, and have them come to the classroom to talk about their trip. They could also answer questions that students have prepared in advance.

6. Have students do research about why Britain decided to send its prisoners to Australia and why they decided to stop this practice.

Resource Information About Tasmania

• Tasmania—"the other island," as Tasmanians describe it—is located about 150 miles across the Bass Strait from mainland Australia. It has one percent of Australia's land and is mostly forested. Being at about 42 degrees south latitude, its climate is cool and temperate. It has four distinct seasons, with snow in the mountains in the winter and in summer warm, but not hot, temperature. The last ice age ended less than 20,000 years ago, so there are many areas of Tasmania that show the effects of that ice cover. More than 30 percent of Tasmania is included in World Heritage areas, national parks, and reserves. For this reason, Tasmania has become a special destination for bushwalkers, rafters, and fishermen who want to experience this special wilderness.

- Being isolated from continental Australia has meant that there are many plants and animals that are found only in Tasmania. The Huon pine (a tree that lives for an extremely long time), the Tasmanian wolf (an animal now virtually extinct), and the popular Tasmanian devil are examples of this isolation. In Australia as a whole there are more marsupials than in any other place in the world. The wallaby, kangaroo, echidna, and wombat have caught the imagination of many people and provide a rich area of study for students.

- Being in the Southern Hemisphere, Tasmanian seasons are the opposite of Northern Hemisphere seasons. Winter falls in June, July, and August, while summer falls in December, January, and February.

- The population of Tasmania is just about 452,000 people. Hobart, the most populous and the capital city, has 180,000 people. It is Australia's second oldest city. Ocean liners come into the harbor, and it is the destination for the famous Sydney-Hobart Yacht Race held each year in late December.

- Though not a center for industry, Tasmanians make their living from forests, mining, fishing, and a solid tourist industry.

- Australia is a member of Britain's Commonwealth, and it officially recognizes Queen Elizabeth II as its monarch. It is a federal parliamentary state, has an elected prime minister, and has a 76-seat Senate and 148-seat House of Representatives. However, there is a constitutional convention scheduled to decide whether Australia will abandon the monarchy and move to a republican system of government.

- Tasmania has a State Parliament with a 35-member House of Assembly and a 19-member Legislative Council. The premier is the head of government, and the governor is the designated representative of the Queen.

Bibliography

Alexander, Alison. *Tasmania's Colonial Years.* Sydney, Australia: Hodder and Stoughton, 1986. (Children's literature)

Brody, Anne Marie, ed. *Stories: Eleven Aboriginal Artists.* Sydney, Australia: Craftsman House, 1997.

Daly, Margo, Anne Dehne, David Leffman, and Chris Scott. *Australia: The Rough Guide.* London: Penguin Books, 1997.

Doubilet, David. "Beneath the Tasman Sea." *National Geographic,* Vol. 191 (January 1997), pp. 82–101.

Finkel, George. *Tasmania, 1803–1900.* West Melbourne: Nelson, 1976. (Children's literature)

Finley, Hugh, et. al. *Australia.* Oakland, CA: Lonely Planet Publications, 1996.

Gouldthorpe, Peter. *The Child's Guide To Tasmania: A Travelling Companion.* Launceston, Tasmania: Regal, 1989. (Children's literature)

Harder, Bentsion. ed. *Let's Go Australia.* New York: St. Martin's Press, 1998.

Hopkins, David. *The Convict Era: Port Arthur Chains of Discipline. Book 2.* Devonport, Tasmania: Taswegia, 1993.

Hughes, Robert. *The Fatal Shore: The Epic of Australia's Founding.* New York: Vintage Books, 1986.

Kelly, Ian, and Leigh Miller. eds. *Living In Tasmania.* Toorak, Australia: Tasmanian Geography Teacher's Association, 1986. (Children's literature)

Odgeis, Sally. *Tasmania: A Guide.* Cincinnati: Kangaroo Press (distributed by Seven Hills Book Distributers), 1989.

O'Neill, Judith. *Transported to Van Diemen's Land: The Story of Two Convicts.* Cambridge: Cambridge University Press, 1977. (Children's literature)

Renwick, George. *A Fair Go For All: Australian/American Interactions.* Yarmouth, Maine: Intercultural Press, 1991.

Robinson, Carl. *Australia: The Island Continent.* Chicago: Passport Books, 1994.

World Wide Web Sites

http://www.tas.gov.au

http://www.tasmania.com

http://www.tased.edu.au/library/links/kids.htm

http://www.parks.tas.gov.au/tpws.html

http://www.utas.edu.au/docs/zoology/profiles.html

Exercise 21

Map of Tasmania and Australia

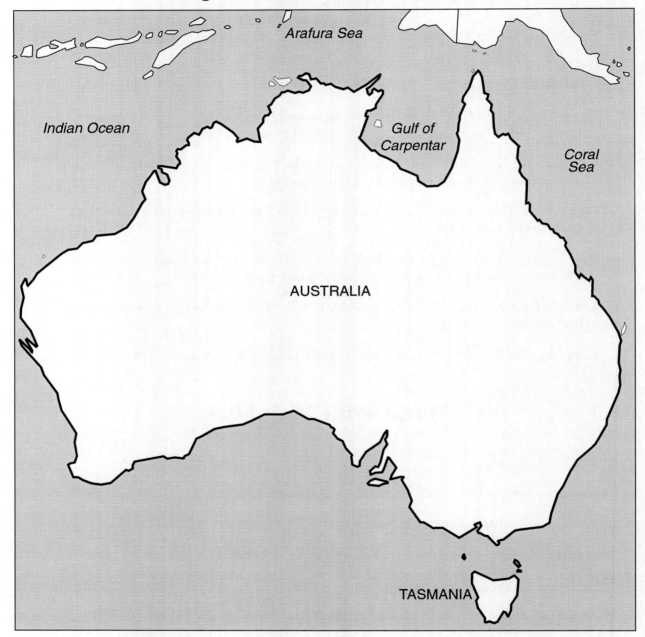

Arafura Sea

Indian Ocean

Gulf of
Carpentar

Coral
Sea

AUSTRALIA

TASMANIA

Exercise 22

Two Tasmanian Families—Cultural Features

Food	Rules and Penalties
Clothing	Type of Government
Housing	Transportation
Language	Education
Religion	Other Special Features

       Comparing Cultures

Exercise 23

Initial E-mail Contact

Tuesday, February 22, 10:15 A.M.

From: Harding@ctr.sch.edu.au
Subject: Tasmanian devil
To: Robyn Everett

I am writing a paper about the Tasmanian devil, so my cousin Ann Harding, whom you met during the summer, suggested that I contact you. She said your mother did something with Australian animals at the University of Tasmania. Can you or she help me find information about the Tasmanian devil? Once late at night my family heard several devils growling over something they had killed. It sure sounded scary.

Thanks for your help. I live on our family's hop farm outside New Norfolk, by the way.

Gary Harding.

Wednesday, February 24, 5:00 P.M.

From: Everett@utas.edu.au
Re: Information about the Tasmanian devil
To: Gary Harding

Hi. I remember your cousin Ann. I met her at the Salmon Ponds fish hatchery in Plenty. Both our families were in the building where the salmon and trout eggs hatch, and I mentioned how much I like to eat the trout my father catches. Ann said she liked the salmon better. So we talked for awhile about what we liked to eat. We both agreed that the huge crayfish (lobster) was our favorite. Did you know that trout and salmon have been raised here since 1864?

I can give you lots of information about the Tasmanian devil. My mother is an Associate Professor of Zoology at the University of Tasmania and has studied the Tasmanian devil. I am using her computer in her office now. She said that the Zoology Department has a website and that you can print out material on the Tasmanian devil from that website. They also have lots of other animals listed. The site is: http:www.utas.edu.au/docs/zoology/profiles.html.

(continued)

Exercise 23

Initial E-mail Contact *(continued)*

Several times I have gone along with my mother when she has been collecting data about the Tasmanian devil. I agree that its scream is scary, but my mother says that it is usually only out hunting at night and keeps well back in the dense vegetation. I am thinking that once I finish high school, I will go to the University of Tasmania and study to be a zoologist.

I don't know much about how hops grow, would you tell me something about that? Isn't this the time that they are harvested?

Robyn Everett

Friday, February 26, 10:30 A.M.

From: Harding@ctr.sch.edu.au
Subject: Our farm
To: Robyn Everett

Hi. Thanks for the information. I have gotten the information from the zoology website. That helped me a lot. The thing that I was most interested in is how the Tasmanian devil's pink ears turn purple when it is agitated. That would be something to see! My family is going to go to the Bonorong Park Wildlife Center this weekend and look at the Tasmanian devils they have there. I figure I will learn a lot more by seeing them.

Our farm is located about 10 miles from New Norfolk in the Bushy Park area. My great grandfather had this farm, and it has stayed in our family ever since. We have a big, white two-story farmhouse, and my sister and I each have our own room. Near the house is a large barn with drying kilns. When we harvest the hops, they have to be dried. We plant the hops plants next to very high strings, and as they grow, they climb the strings. When the plants reach the top of the strings, they spread out along wires that are connected so that the hops grow horizontally. The top layer is about 18 feet high. In the fall we harvest the crop and take it to the barns for drying.

(continued)

Exercise 23

Initial E-mail Contact *(continued)*

I help out with planting, keeping the weeds out, and harvesting. We have to work very hard on the harvesting because there is just a very short time to get the crop in while it is at its prime. Some years it is very dry, and we don't get as good a crop. All of our crop is bought by Tasmanian Breweries in Hobart, where it is used to make beer.

Coming up in several weeks is the New Norfolk Hop Festival. There will be lots of people coming from all over Tasmania to attend that. I always enjoy that each year, as there is always lots to eat and things to see.

Do you live right in Hobart? The teacher is checking to see that we are busy on school-related work. Better sign off now.

Gary Harding

Arthur Circus—Hobart

Sunday, February 28, 3:00 P.M.

From: Everett@utas.edu.au
Re: Where we live
To: Gary Harding

Hi. I came into work with Mom. She needed to put together some notes for her zoology class tomorrow. I was glad to know more about growing hops. This sure is a busy time for you.

We live in the Battery Park area of Hobart. Actually, if you know that area, we are just a block away from Arthur Circus. Arthur Circus is that circle of about 10 houses around a small central park. The houses are almost all built the same, except for the different colors. I'll ask Dad why it is called Arthur Circus. He sells real estate and would know the history of our area.

Got to go; write me when you have gotten to see the Tasmanian devil.

Robyn

  Comparing Cultures

Exercise 24

E-mail Contact a Week Later

Monday, March 8, 11:00 A.M.

From: Harding@ctr.sch.edu.au
Subject: A live Tasmanian devil
To: Robyn Everett

Hi, Robyn. My family and I went to the Bonorong Park Wildlife Center Saturday and saw the Tasmanian devil. Wow, has he ever got a lot of teeth! He was chewing on the carcass of some animal and making such strange noises. He seemed to be able to crush the bones as though they were carrots. The material from your mom helped me tell my family lots of things about him. Thanks.

In our social studies class, we have been studying about the early prisoners that came to Australia. Our teacher asked us to begin planning a class trip to Port Arthur to see the remains of the old penal settlement there. I have never been there and am not sure how interesting it will be. I am glad it will still be warm when we are there, so wearing my jeans and a shirt should be enough. I imagine it was really cold there in the winter time, being so close to the water. Have you been there?

I talked to my dad about growing hops in this area, and he said that they have grown hops here since about 1864. In the beginning they had lots of trouble finding the right variety of hops that would grow in this climate. We have a microclimate in this area that provides just the right amount of rain and sun. I didn't know much about the early years of growing hops, so Dad gave me some material from the Oast House Museum in New Norfolk that I am looking over.

What do you do after school, besides go to your mother's office at the university?

Gary

Tuesday, March 9, 4:30 P.M.

From: Everett@utas.edu.au
Re: After school
To: Gary Harding

Oast House—Bushy Park

(continued)

Exercise 24

E-mail Contact a Week Later *(continued)*

Hi, Gary. Most of the time I go home and do my homework. My sister, who is younger, and I share the same room, so sometimes that is a problem. She likes to put on music that seems so juvenile to me. I have a hard time concentrating. Sometimes I just go for walks around our neighborhood. Remember I said I would ask my father about how Arthur Circus got its name? Well, he told me that the circle was named for Lieutenant-Governor Arthur, an early organizer of prison life in Tasmania. Many of the the homes in Battery Point in the early days were made for fishing families.

Our class is going on a field trip too, but not so far away. We are going to Parliament House Thursday. Our teacher says that is the best day to go because the House of Assembly meets at 11:00 that day to ask and respond to questions about current policies. I have seen the outside of the building but have not been inside. We are busy studying all about our government. I doubt whether we will see the premier, but maybe we will be able to talk with some of the members of the Legislative Council. I'll let you know how that tour goes.

The information about growing hops is interesting. I have not seen the hops farms. Will you work on the farm after you finish your schooling?

I have to go now; Mom is ready to go home, and I have to help fix supper. We are having a barbecue for some of Dad's clients. Mom says on the way home we can buy lamington to serve for dessert. Which do you like best about the outside of the cake, the chocolate covering or the coconut covering? I guess it doesn't much matter, as you have to eat them both at once. I do like coconut best though.

Robyn

Thursday, March 10, 11:00 A.M.

From: Harding@ctr.sch.edu.au
Subject: Port Arthur
To: Robyn Everett

Hi, Robyn. I have a great idea. Could you come out to see our farm? Mom says your whole family could come, and we would show you around the farm. Perhaps we could all go down to the Oast House Museum. Let me know.

(continued)

     Comparing Cultures

Exercise 24

E-mail Contact a Week Later *(continued)*

Our trip to Port Arthur is scheduled next Monday. There is a Tasmanian Devil Park on the way to Port Arthur, and some of us have talked the class into including that on our trip. Have you been to that one? They have lots of other animals there too, and part of it is a wildlife rescue center. I really would rather see that than spend lots of time walking through some old prison buildings.

Got to go. The teacher is giving me the eye.

Gary

Salamanca Market—Hobart

Friday, March 12, 4:42 P.M.

From: Everett@utas.edu.au
Re: Port Arthur
To: Gary Harding

Hi, Gary. My sister was making so much noise I decided to come here to study. Yes, I have been to the Tasmanian Devil Park and also to Port Arthur. I didn't think I would like Port Arthur before I went, but once I got there, it was really something. The treatment of the prisoners was horrible, and many of them were not allowed to see or talk to anyone else. When they went to chapel, they had to stand in stalls with sides so high that the prisoners could see only the pulpit. They were allowed to sing hymns together, which was the only time during the week they could talk. I'm glad that time is over.

Our trip to Parliament House was OK. I got tired of hearing people talk on and on. However, I could see many adults who seemed to be very involved. Perhaps it is an adult thing. What do you think? Everybody seemed to be so serious. We were given a talk by one of the guides about how laws are made.

I told my family about your invitation to come out to your farm. We can't do that this weekend, as we have a canoeing trip scheduled. What about the next weekend? I could have my mom call your mom and talk about the details. It will be fun to meet you. Write you later.

Robyn

Activity 8. Asante Family

Introduction

The dilemma faced by Kofi—whether to apprentice with his *kente*-cloth-making father or gain further schooling and leave his home town—resonates with the basic decisions made by children everywhere. However, in Ghana, and the Asante culture in particular, this pull between the traditional and the new is part of the fabric of every person's life. The Asante are a people with a rich cultural heritage going back many centuries. Their struggle to maintain what is uniquely theirs takes place amid the increasing presence of computers, television, multinational companies, and cellular telephones.

Objectives

1. To have students discover and record the major features of the culture of present-day Asante peoples in the country of Ghana

2. To develop students' ability to identify in another culture examples of traditions, customs, values, and technology

Time to complete

A minimum of three class sessions, with more time required if supplementary activities are undertaken

```
┌─────────────────────────────────────────────────────────────────┐
│                          Materials                                │
│                                                                   │
│   •   Exercise 25: Map of Ghana (Get a large map of Africa, too)  │
│   •   Exercise 26: Asante Family—Cultural Features                │
│   •   Exercise 27: Kofi's Dilemma                                 │
│   •   Exercise 28: Kwame Responds                                 │
│   •   Exercise 29: A Museum Director Reaches Out                  │
└─────────────────────────────────────────────────────────────────┘
```

Procedure

1. Use a large class map of Africa to identify the following: Ghana, Togo, Burkina Faso, Ivory Coast, Kumasi, Accra, Tamale, Volta River, Lake Volta, and the Gold Coast. Have students label these countries on Exercise 25. Then have them compare the size of western Africa with that of the United States. Since Ghana is located close to the equator, have the students predict what climate and vegetation they would expect to find there.

2. Distribute to students Exercise 26: Asante Family—Cultural Features. Then ask each group to read together Exercise 27: Kofi's Dilemma. When they have finished, have them write their answers on Exercise 26.

3. When the groups have finished this activity, ask all students to write down on paper two reasons why they might want to leave their home town after they finish their education and two reasons why they might want to stay. Conduct a class discussion about their reasons for going and staying. Then ask the class to respond to the statement: I would urge/discourage Kofi to plan to leave his home town because . . .

4. Have members of each group read together Exercise 28: Kwame Responds. When they have finished, have them write the appropriate information on Exercise 26. Have all groups share their information and make sure additional information is put into the worksheet.

5. Read aloud Exercise 29: A Museum Director Reaches Out. Have students record the relevant information on Exercise 26. Divide the class into four small groups. Have each group discuss and then write an answer to one of assigned four questions: (1) What bias might the museum director have about Kofi's decision? (2) Will Kofi's creative urges be unfulfilled if he continues his formal education? (3) Why do you think Kofi's father is leaving the decision up to Kofi? (4) What advice might Kofi's mother be wanting to offer? Conduct a class discussion about the answers of each group.

Suggestions for Further Study of Ghana

- Slave trading was centered in western Africa. Have students do research about who engaged in this trade, how this trade was carried out, where the slaves went, and the factors that brought the trade to an end. Oral reports could be made to the whole class.

- Have small groups of students select areas of Ghana other than the Asante area. They should focus their attention on the specific climate of that region and how that climate influences what people do for a living. Ask them to present their findings in a poster. Take class time to view each group's poster.

- Create a bulletin board about current happenings in Ghana. Newspaper clippings and material gathered from Web sites could be posted daily for students to read.

- Invite to your classroom people who have lived or visited in Ghana. Have students prepare questions in advance of their visit, and have them conduct the interview with the visitor(s). Ask the visitor to bring to the class clothing, folk art, and other things that would allow students to know more about Ghana.

- Investigate whether there is a museum close by that would have African holdings, particularly from Ghana. Arrange to visit the museum or to have a traveling exhibit sent for use in your class. Sometimes museum personnel will visit a class, bringing with them artifacts to view.

- Asante people have many holidays and cultural celebrations. Learn about a celebration, and then stage that celebration in your class. The Adae festival, written about in the letter from Kofi to his brother, would be fun to stage in class. The students could make paper costumes that look like *kente* cloth, create staffs with gold-plated tops, and make the golden stool for display next to the asantehene. They could also make supplies of gold jewelry for important people to wear.

Resource Information about the Asante and Ghana

- The country of Ghana is located on the west coast of the African continent, next to the Côte d'Ivoire, Burkina Faso, and Togo. It is about the same size as Great Britain or the state of Oregon. It is located between 5 and 10 degrees north latitude and has three climactic zones. The Asante, who number over 2 million people, are located near the center of the country. They are part of the largest ethnic group, the Akan, which is about 44 percent of the population. The second largest city in Ghana, Kumasi, is located within this group. Kumasi is a modern city with about 385,000 people. Bonwire is a suburb of Kumasi.

- Ghana has a population of about 18 million people, of whom virtually all are black African. They are divided into more than 100 ethnic groups, each sharing a common language and cultural heritage. Social interaction is often limited between the groups, and although significant tension often exists, violence is rare. In large cities, different groups live in their own section. English is the official language of Ghana, due both to Britain's earlier colonial presence and to the fact that there needs to be a single language that doesn't disadvantage some ethnic groups.

- Nearly 70 percent of Ghanaians earn their living from fishing or from farming, timber, or other agriculturally related jobs. Extended families live in rural compounds, where the oldest male is the head of the family. Many relatives live in the compound, and all who are able help with the farming. Traditional village ways are increasingly threatened by people who go away to the cities for work and later return to resume life in the family's rural compound or in the village or small town.

- Around 1700 A.D., after many years of fighting with neighboring tribes, the Asante, under the leadership of King Osei, united the tribes into one Asante nation. The city of Kumasi was established, and trade was initiated with the Dutch and English in the area. They also expanded their trade with the peoples to the north of present-day Ghana. The Asante continued to dominate the region the Europeans called the Gold Coast for close to 200 years. In 1874 the British took charge of the Gold Coast and sought to control the Asante king for the next 24 years. Finally, in 1900 they deposed the king and defeated the Asante through fierce fighting in the jungle. The Gold Coast was run as a British colony until independence in 1957.

    Ghana, as the newly independent nation was called, became the first African colony to gain independence from Britain. In 1960 the country became a republic, and Kwame Nkrumah was elected president. In 1966 Nkrumah was deposed by a military coup. In 1969 elections were held, but the military took over again in 1972. In 1979 Flight Lieutenant Jerry Rawlings overthrew the government. He served for a time without elections and then, with elections, for two terms. Upon the expiration of his term in 2000, he would no longer be eligible to serve. In 1992 a national assembly was established, and a constitution was adopted.

- Whether or not a family has a religious affiliation with the Christian or Muslim faith, traditional African beliefs and practices have considerable influence on how people live. The Supreme Being, who has created all things and given power to living and nonliving things, is approached through intermediaries. These include the spirits of ancestors and special animate and inanimate objects. This traditional faith also includes belief in magic potions, witches, and wizards. Various rituals are performed by the family at important times, like birth, puberty, marriage, and death. Certain people in the community have special powers to communicate with this spirit world.

Bibliography

Ardouin, Claude, and Emmanuel Arinze, eds. *Museums and the Community in West Africa.* Washington, DC: Smithsonian Institution Press, 1995.

Beckwith, Carol. "Fantasy Coffins in Ghana." *National Geographic,* Vol.186 (September 1994), pp. 120–130.

_____. "Royal Gold of the Asante Empire." *National Geographic,* Vol. 190 (October 1996), pp. 36–47.

Boateng, Faustine. *Asante.* New York: Rosen Publishing Group, Inc., 1996. (Children's literature)

Chou, Daniel, and Elliott Skinner. *A Glorious Age in Africa: The Story of Three Great African Empires.* Trenton, NJ: African World Press, 1990.

Edgerton, Robert. *The Fall of the Asante Empire.* New York: Free Press, 1995.

Grindal, Bruce. *Growing Up in Two Worlds: Education and Transition Among the Sisala of Northern Ghana.* New York: Holt, Rinehard, and Winston, 1972.

Hintz, Martin. *Ghana.* Chicago: Children's Press, 1987. (Children's literature)

Hudgens, Jim, and Richard Trillo. *Africa.* London: Rough Guides, Ltd., 1995.

Koslow, Philip. *Asante: The Gold Coast.* New York: Chelsea House Publishers, 1996. (Children's literature)

McKissack, Patricia, and Fredrick McKissack. *The Royal Kingdoms of Ghana, Mali, and Songhay.* New York: Henry Holt and Company, 1994. (Children's literature)

Nugent, Paul. *Big Men, Small Boys and Politics in Ghana.* New York: Pinter, 1995.

Nwanunobi, C.O. *Soninke.* New York: Rosen Publishing Group, Inc., 1996. (Children's literature)

Okeke, Chika. *Fante.* New York: Rosen Publishing Group, Inc., 1998. (Children's literature)

Strathern, Oona. *Traveller's Literary Companions: Africa.* Chicago: Passport Books, 1995.

World Wide Web Sites

http://www.geographica.com/ghana/

http://www.ghana.com.republic/education/educationl.html/

http://www.ghanaforum.com/

http://www.interknowledge.com/ghana/index.html

http://www.erols.com/kemet/kente.htm
   (Excellent on kente cloth)

http://members.aol.com/davilojo/dl.htm
   (Excellent on kente cloth)

Name _____ Date _____

Exercise 25

Map of Western Africa and Ghana

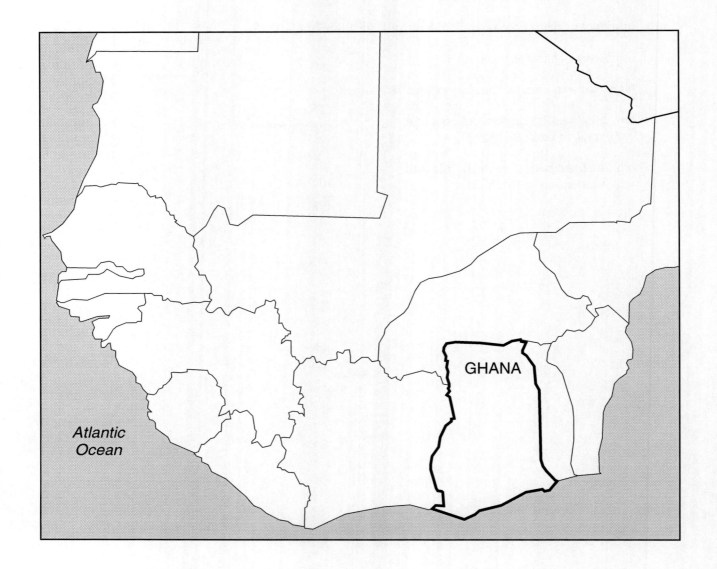

Atlantic
Ocean

GHANA

         Comparing Cultures

Exercise 26

Asante Family—Cultural Features

Food	Rules and Penalties
Clothing	Type of Government
Housing	Transportation
Language	Education
Religion	Other Special Features

Exercise 27

Kofi's Dilemma

Bonwire, Ghana

October 5, 1999

Dear Kwame,

Yesterday, our school class went to the Ghana National Cultural Center in Kumasi. We saw many things, including displays of *kente* cloth like the ones that Father weaves. His work is just as good as what was on display. I said that to the museum director, who was giving us a tour. He urged me to become a *kente* weaver like Father. He said that our nation needs young people to continue the traditions that have been in existence for hundreds of years.

I am feeling so confused. I like to work with Father after school. He has been teaching me how to weave, and I am getting very good. I love to learn about the stories that each design tells. But I don't know whether I want to spend the rest of my life weaving. You learned how to weave but continued your schooling. Now you are a government worker in Accra. I think I would like that, too. Father wants me to work more with him, but he says the decision is up to me. What do you think I should do?

I am writing this at home just before supper. I can smell the palm nut soup and fried ripe plantain that mother is fixing. Yesterday, at the market Mother got some sun-dried fish, and we will be having that soon. I still like to go with Mother to the market and see the mounds of coconuts and pineapples. Living in Accra, do you get these things?

I remember when you returned home and we all went to the Akwasidae Kese festival in Kumasi. I sure wish we could have been at the Manhyia Palace to see Asantehene, our king, offer the food and drink to the ancestors. I understand that only the most important people are invited, but Father is important because he makes the *kente* cloth that is used to make the robes that many of these people wear. What I like the most about the festival is seeing the Asantehene parade by with all of his leaders around him. I don't see how he can move with all that gold he wears. Then the singing and dancing are fun, too. I am so glad you came back for that special day. Mother was so happy to see you.

(continued)

Exercise 27

Kofi's Dilemma *(continued)*

In school we are learning about the early history of Ghana. Our teacher told us about how the high priest, Okomfo Anokye, created a Golden Stool that was used to unite the tribes under the Asante Asantehene Osei Tutu around 1700 A.D. The part of the story I liked best was learning that the name of the stool was Siki Dwa Kofi, the Golden Stool Born on Friday. I was born on Friday, too. We have to write a report about the present-day government of Ghana. I do know that there are 10 regions and 110 administrative districts. They use government funds to run schools, help with health care, and help farmers with their crops. I also know that there is a Parliament with 200 seats. Do you have any contact with people in Parliament? Can you send me some information about that and about our president?

Did you remember that our cousin Adwoa is also in my class? I know that Uncle Kwakou does not see any reason for her to go to school, since she will get married and have a family. She spends a lot of time after school helping with the younger children and preparing things for our supper. She is getting very good at making the hot pepper sauce to serve with the boiled yams and cassava. When you get married, will you want your wife to work? I know that Aunt Afua wanted to continue in school to learn to be a teacher, but her father would not allow it. Our teacher grew up here in Bonwire and took a teacher training course after she finished her junior secondary school. She keeps encouraging all the girls to continue their education.

I am glad that the rains are almost over. I get tired of so much rain, and Father can't do his weaving in the courtyard. When it gets really hot, though, I remember the rain and wish it were here.

I look forward to hearing from you.

Kofi

Drying groundnuts—Fihini village

         Comparing Cultures

Exercise 28

Kwame Responds

Accra, Ghana

October 12, 1999

Dear Kofi,

I was pleased to get your long letter. I think that is the longest letter you have
ever written me. I know exactly what you are trying to figure out, because I had to
decide what to do in that situation, too. You know what my decision was, but you
don't know why. I loved reading and learning everything I could in school. When I
would work with Father to weave, I couldn't wait to finish so I could get back to my
books. I did well in school, and my teachers kept encouraging me to work hard to
pass the exams to get into college. I am very glad I did, because I am very happy
with my work.

When I came home for the Akwasidae Kese festival, I watched you weaving
with Father. You were excited about the patterns you were creating and proud of
your work. I think you have a deep sense of respect for our heritage that I did not
have at your age. All that is to say that I think you would be wise not to decide
anything definite yet. Let more time pass. You will know what to do when you
really have to make a decision. In the meantime, study hard and weave hard.

Some of the foods you mentioned I could get here if I wanted to cook a lot for
myself. Living by myself, I don't do much cooking. I often go to a chop bar where
I can sit outside and eat with others. The food doesn't taste like what mother fixes,
though. I do have the beef with vegetables and eat lots of rice dishes. I haven't had
a coconut for a long time.

You asked when I was going to get married. I haven't found a woman yet that
I want to marry. I would like her to be trained to do work outside the family, and it is
harder to find a woman who does that. I did like a nurse for a while, but we didn't
continue seeing each other. At an earlier time in our country, parents selected who
you would marry. I would find that hard to accept. How about you? Would you
want to marry someone who was picked out for you?

I am putting some written material about Parliament in this letter. I got it when
I was at Parliament yesterday, talking with the representative from our home area
near Kumasi. He was pleased that your school is asking you to learn more about
Parliament. I think you will find the material helpful. There are several things you
should know before you read the material. The National Democratic Congress has

(continued)

Exercise 28

Kwame Responds *(continued)*

the most members, and the main opposition party is the New Patriotic Party. President Rawlings was elected by popular vote. He cannot run again when his term ends in 2000 because he will have been president for two terms of four years, which is as long as our constitution allows. Our constitution was adopted in 1992. There is also a Supreme Court with a Chief Justice and at least four other justices.

You remember that I work as a clerk in the Ministry of Health. I work for an official who helps some of the members of Parliament write laws to help people get better health care. There is still a huge problem with malaria and AIDS, and we think Parliament can do more than it is doing now to help with that. Also we are trying to get our local officials to fund projects to create safe drinking water. There are so many intestinal diseases that come from impure water, and many children your age are sick a lot. You are fortunate that our family has safe drinking water. I think my job is important, and sometimes I can see where there is some real change.

While I like living in Accra, I don't very often get out of the city. I do enjoy seeing people from many other countries. Sometimes, I go to the Ambassador Hotel and sit in the lobby. I see people from places like Sierra Leone, Nigeria, Morocco, England, and America. I like to look at the different ways they dress. Usually, I wear slacks and a shirt, but occasionally I like to put on my *kente* cloth robe and look like a traditional Asante. Sometimes, I see women wearing the *kente* cloth skirt, blouse, and head scarf and am reminded that Mother often wears that. I do miss all of you.

Write to me soon.

Kwame

Dance festival in Ghana

Comparing Cultures

Exercise 29

A Museum Director Reaches Out

Kumasi, Ghana
October 15, 1999

Dear Kofi,

I have been thinking a lot about our conversation when you were in the museum several weeks ago. You seemed so proud of your father's work and knew so well how creative the work was. You recognized so many of the traditional designs and could see how much work went into weaving the finest cloth. I was struck by your enthusiasm and interest.

As a director of a museum, I talk with many artisans and know how dedicated they are to keeping their craft alive. But there are fewer and fewer young people learning these crafts. If we don't have new people learning, our nation of Ghana will lose a very rich part of its life. Therefore, I want to urge you to continue to work with your father to learn how to weave the finest quality *kente* cloth.

Neither you nor your father will know how creative you can become until you have worked for many years. All during the time you are in school, keep working with your father, so later on you can make a decision about whether to continue your studies or leave school to work full time as a *kente* weaver.

Long ago, you would not have had the chance to go to school. You would have become a weaver because your father was a weaver. Now, it is different, and more difficult for you because you have to attend school. It is even harder for your father and mother. They want you to do what you think is best, while at the same time wanting you to continue a rich tradition that has been in your family for a very long time. You have a big decision ahead of you.

I am very proud of our Ghana National Cultural Center. We have been working with many people to build up this center ever since it started over 40 years ago. The museum that you went through with your class was one of our first buildings. We would like to have the Golden Stool here, but that is kept by the Asantehene at the Palace. But we do have the silver stool, which is one of our most prized possessions. The story goes that the King of the Denkyira was sitting on that stool playing a game with his wife when the Asante army killed him and overcame his army. From that time on, the people of that area were part of the Asante territory. This stool is almost three hundred years old. It is important that we know about our earliest beginnings, and some of these objects help us understand our past.

(continued)

Exercise 29

A Museum Director Reaches Out

(continued)

Many of the children who visit here live in Kumasi and not in the small villages that were so common at an earlier time. That is why we created the model of the traditional home that you saw here. We didn't make the walls and floor of mud and the roof of thatch, because we wanted the exhibit to last longer. Nor did we have room to make the compound as large as many family compounds, but we were able to show how three or four generations lived together. Many of the pots and dishes that you saw in our exhibit are probably similar to the ones your family uses today. Some things are the same and some are different.

I hope you will come to the museum again. I would like to talk with you again, and I urge you to take pride in the work of your father—perhaps the work that you will do as well.

Sincerely,

Dr. Gilbert Afrania

Family compound in Tamale

Activity 9. We Do Things the Same, We Do Things Differently

Introduction

It is at this point that significant gains can be made in understanding the sources of cultural diversity. In order to discover factors influencing a group's behavior, students can examine two major bodies of information: the various foods and clothing styles of each culture.

Objectives

1. To increase the students' knowledge of similarities and differences among all the cultures studied

2. To develop students' ability to identify in each culture factors influencing specific behaviors and beliefs

Time to complete

Two class periods

Materials

- Exercises 2, 4, 9, 13, 17, 22, and 26 (completed)
- Exercise 30: Similarities and Differences
- Exercise 31: Factors Influencing Cultural Development

Procedure

1. Have students meet in their cooperative learning groups. Make sure students have on their desks the Unit I activities from each culture they have studied.

2. Distribute to each student Exercise 30: Similarities and Differences.

3. Have students look at the category *food* on all of the activities and find items that are the same or very similar in all the cultures. They should list those items on Exercise 30 under the category *similar*. They then list items that are not similar under the category *different*. If all six of the other cultures have been studied, it may be helpful to list similarities for three or more cultures, noting which cultures share the same item. Students should complete each category in Exercise 30 using the same procedure.

4. After a short time, have students stop work and read aloud some of their findings. Make sure all students are following the correct procedure, and then ask them to return to their work.

5. When the students have completed their task, have them go back to the category *food* on Exercise 30 and list under *factors* several influences on the kinds of food that are eaten in each culture.

6. For this exercise, refer to Exercise 31: Factors Influencing Cultural Development. You can use it in two ways: either as a teacher guide to help students add to their list of factors that determine types of foods eaten in other cultures, or as a handout that students can search through to discover factors they have missed.

7. Follow the same procedure with the category *clothing*. If time allows, finish all categories on Exercise 30 and conduct a short review of possible reasons for differences in cultures. If more time is available, one or more of the following supplemental activities can be done.

Supplemental Activities

- Often when one factor in a culture changes, adjustments in the way things are done need to be made. As a class or in cooperative learning groups, decide what adjustments might be necessary in the following situations:

  (a) Annual rainfall dropping from 35 to 10 inches

  (b) North Korea and South Korea becoming reunited

  (c) More than 40 percent of the citizens of the United States speaking Spanish

- Make a list of items of food and clothing that originated in other countries but are now a regular part of American culture.

Exercise 30

Similarities and Differences

Similar	*Different*	*Factors*
Food		
Clothing		
Housing		
Language		
Religion		

(continued)

Comparing Cultures

Name _____ Date _____

Exercise 30

Similarities and Differences (continued)

Similar	Different	Factors
Rules and Penalties		
Type of Government		
Transportation		
Education		
Other Special Features		

   Comparing Cultures

Exercise 31

Factors Influencing Cultural Development

Food

- Condition of the soil
- Length of growing period
- Amount of rain and sun
- Presence and availability of breeding stock (animals) or seeds (plants)
- Altitude
- Type of food considered acceptable to eat (Religious practice sometimes rules for or against certain foods.)
- Cost of producing or importing the food
- Availability of fertilizers and pesticides
- Level of technology

Clothing

- Raw materials available
- Ease with which raw materials or the finished product can be imported
- Amount of money necessary to process and manufacture the raw material
- Level of technology
- Types of clothing items considered acceptable to wear
- Traditions regarding the use of clothing
- Skill of persons making the clothing
- Designs and patterns available

Housing

- Climate
- Raw materials available
- Level of technology
- Traditions regarding the kinds of houses used
- Amount of money available to spend
- Ability to import materials
- Craftsmanship needed to produce a particular kind of house

Language

- Spoken or written language of the previous generation
- Number of different cultures in the same area
- Opportunities for schooling in languages
- Government role in determining which language is the official language

Religion

- Beliefs and rituals of the previous generation
- Extent to which other religions have penetrated the culture
- Degree to which people actually practice their religion
- Presence of governments or groups hostile to religion

(continued)

Exercise 31

Factors Influencing Cultural
Development *(continued)*

Rules and Penalties

- Available religion(s)
- Explicit and implicit behaviors
- Average level of education
- Presence of more than one set of acceptable behaviors

Type of Government

- Religious beliefs
- Traditional political practices
- History of domination by another culture
- Level of economic satisfaction among citizens
- Role of the military

Transportation

- Type of physical terrain
- Technology level
- Type of transportation considered acceptable
- Money available to pay for transportation
- Degree of contact with forms of transportation in other cultures
- Need to travel to support acceptable lifestyle

Education

- Degree to which it is valued
- Past educational practices
- Economic conditions
- Quantity of information and values to be passed on
- Roles of the family, town, state, and nation

Other Special Features

- Presence of extraordinary artistic, scientific, religious, or political talent
- Frequency of cataclysmic physical events, such as earthquakes, floods, famine, drought, sunspot activity, or hurricanes
- War at home or abroad
- Availability of communication technology, such as satellites, television, telephone, and newspaper
- Cultural stance toward contact with foreign visitors or businesses

95      *Comparing Cultures*

UNIT II

Creating a New
Culture

Unit II: Creating a New Culture

An Overview

The overall goals of this unit are to have students gain firsthand experience in creating a culture and to increase their ability to work cooperatively with other students.

In this unit, the primary mode of learning about cultures is small-group interaction. Each cooperative learning group of four students creates its own culture. For this task, it is important that creativity be stressed so that groups create something different from what currently exists. Interaction with other groups in the early stages of this project is discouraged in order to give the groups time to generate their own particular product. Once the groups are well into the activity, they may benefit from interaction with other groups, perhaps finding inspiration to produce interesting modifications of their ideas and products. Some suggested interactions can be found in Activity 13.

The role of the teacher in this process is to help groups resolve any problems resulting from an inability to work cooperatively, to ensure that all students get their ideas heard, and to suggest resources to help the culture groups develop their ideas. As much as possible, the teacher should avoid giving direct suggestions about the creation of a culture. Sometimes it is helpful to give the whole class information in such areas as language codes, math systems, types of decision making, methods used to discourage deviation from accepted practices, or the function of map symbols. Information about such topics is contained in the student exercises that follow each activity.

Encourage the groups to use the special talents of all members. Some students may be attracted to the more abstract tasks of creating a language or math system, whereas others may be drawn to making clothes, constructing models of transportation, communicating with other groups, or developing maps. The more students work together on group tasks, the more all members will feel they are becoming an integral part of the new culture.

At the end of each work session on their culture, each group should use Exercise 39 to record the work that was done, any unresolved group problems, the percentage of time each member worked on the project, and requests for special assistance from the teacher. This exercise should be turned in to the teacher to serve as a record of the needs and progress of the group.

This unit can be used as infrequently as once a week and still retain its impact. Nevertheless, it is designed to be used over a five- to six-week period of time with two to three exercises per week. This schedule enables students to do most of the work in class but provides time for ambitious students to work outside of class to develop their culture more thoroughly.

Unit II: Creating a New Culture

Activity 10. Getting Started

Introduction

Introduce students to the entire project, giving them time to understand what they will be doing. Once they have achieved the necessary understanding of the project, they will start creating their own culture.

Objectives

1. To give students an understanding of the overall unit and specific directions for making their own culture

2. To strengthen students' ability to work together with people whose ideas and interests are diverse

Time to complete

One class period

Materials

- Exercise 32: Culture Project
- The following materials can be used throughout the entire unit: large poster board for culture map, markers, crayons, paints, clay, fabric, Popsicle sticks, pipe cleaners, construction paper, and any other materials deemed useful. (Recognize that materials supplied to all groups are, in effect, "raw materials"; later on, the class can investigate how each group used the same raw materials.)

Procedure

1. Form new cooperative learning groups of four students. Make sure each group has a good mix of academic, social, and leadership skills. There should also be a balanced mix of girls and boys in each group.

2. Arrange a common work surface and area for each group.

3. Review the things that the class learned in Unit 1 and explain that each group is going to create its own culture. Emphasize that the final product will be something that has not existed before, so the content of the culture will be entirely determined by the group. Conduct a short brainstorming session to aid the students in thinking about things that don't exist now. An example of how this session might be conducted follows.

   Operating as a whole class, with the teacher writing ideas on the board, the students supply examples of ways in which people in their new culture might differ in physical appearance from themselves. (In brainstorming, remember to make no negative or evaluative statements about another's suggestions. This procedure is used strictly for the purpose of generating new ideas.)

   > *Examples:* Head at the bottom of the body, two heads, six arms, or eyes where the ears are.

4. Make sure all students understand the task before groups start to work on the material.

5. Have students start working on their own cooperative culture groups. Early decisions the group will have to make include the following:

   • During what time period does the culture exist? (past, present, future)

   • Where is the culture located? (island, current country, outer space, or other)

   • What level of technology will the culture possess?

   • What will be the culture's name?

Name _____ Date _____

Culture Project

Your group is to create an entirely new culture. It can be located anywhere in time and space you wish. In creating your culture, you must develop at a minimum the following materials:

1. A **map** detailing the location of your culture.

   (a) Include the major **physical features** of your location (mountains, cities, hills, swamps, plateaus, plains, rivers, oceans, roads, railroads, airports, other forms of transportation, and any other features that can be shown on a map).

   (b) Devise a **map key** that codes the following: direction, distance, physical features such as vegetation, glaciers, and any other landforms that distinguish your culture.

2. A one-page description of a special **holiday or religious event** held in your culture.

3. At least **two laws** that apply to all inhabitants of your culture, along with a description of the penalties that result when these laws are broken.

4. A **special language**, to be defined by an **alphabet**; the names of 20 things in your culture; 10 action words; and a letter from one person to another. An English translation should be provided for all words created.

   Items 1–4 are due by _____.

5. A **calculating system** showing the following:

   (a) A way to **count** from one to one hundred.

   (b) **Word problems:** five using addition, five using subtraction, and five using multiplication. You may use equivalent functions if you have created them.

6. A minimum of two examples of **clothing** worn by members of your culture. (These can be drawn or made.)

7. A means of **transporting** inhabitants and/or materials. (This can be a drawing or an original model.)

(continued)

Exercise 32

Culture Project *(continued)*

8. A plan detailing how your culture's **traditions** will be passed on to the next generation, along with a listing of 10 things you wish to pass on.

Items 5–8 are due by _____.

9. A **house** (or other method of shelter) used in your culture (drawing or model).

10. Three **tools** used in your culture.

11. An explanation of the method by which members of your culture **resolve serious disagreements with each other**.

12. A complete plan for working out **disagreements with several other cultures**.

13. A form of **government** used in your culture.

Items 9–13 are due by _____.

All things made for your culture should be fairly small to allow for adequate storage space. Feel free to make additional items that express the uniqueness of your culture. These can be presented for extra credit.

Unit II: Creating a New Culture

Activity 11. Expanding the Cultural Options

Introduction

Because of their limited experience with other cultures, students probably will need assistance in creating a culture different from their own. Therefore, the teacher can provide information that will help them make decisions about features such as maps, language, counting system, clothing, government, and problem-solving techniques.

Objectives

1. To increase students' information base and knowledge about diverse practices and customs

2. To help students create the features that will best define their cultures

Time to complete

Each exercise takes approximately 10 minutes to explain. Discussion of the content could follow if desired.

> ### *Materials*
>
> - Exercise 33: Maps and Keys
> - Exercise 34: Language
> - Exercise 35: Calculating System
> - Exercise 36: Clothing
> - Exercise 37: Resolving Differences
> - Exercise 38: Government

Procedure

1. During the second class period, distribute and explain Exercise 33: Maps and Keys. The degree to which the teacher provides explanation depends on the ability of the class to process written material without assistance.

2. Each additional exercise should be distributed and discussed at the appropriate time.

3. Because the unit is designed so that students work on more than one cultural feature at a time, they should be encouraged to share responsibilities for different facets of the culture. Discourage them from all working on one facet of the culture at a time. Pair work is especially effective at this time. Students need to coordinate their work so they can review what each pair has done and make sure that certain facets of their culture are turned in for evaluation on the designated due dates.

4. For any topics treated in the activities, the teacher can display or describe supplemental items that will add depth to the students' treatment of the material.

Exercise 33

Maps and Keys

The following are some suggestions you might keep in mind as you prepare a map and key of the location of your culture.

1. Before you start your own map, look at other maps to see how they are constructed and what kinds of things are put in their keys. The kinds of maps to look at would include topographic, road, political, weather, and vegetation. Use as many ideas from each of these maps as possible.

2. Make your own symbols to represent certain features of your land.

3. Leave room on the map for more features to be added later.

4. Consider the role you want weather to play in your culture. If you want parts of your land to be cold, what would they look like on the map?

5. Include on your map the ways people will get from one place to another. Some possibilities are roads, space shuttle, railroad, trail, or boat. How do you want to show these on the map?

6. Make your map colorful and interesting—it will be the largest feature of your culture on display.

7. Once you have a language, you could label your map and key in that language. Supply a translation.

8. One of the most difficult aspects of map making involves keeping things to scale. You should decide how much distance you want to represent by one inch and keep to that scale throughout the map.

9. Somewhere on your map you will want to indicate the directions like north, south, east, and west. You may decide to call them something else, but there should be some indication of what direction you travel when you go toward the top of your map.

Exercise 34

Language

Keep the following items in mind as you create your own language.

1. Languages give names to actions, attributes, things, ideas, and experiences. A language can use pictures, letters, and sounds to communicate experience and ideas. To learn the language of someone whose culture is different from your own, it is necessary to translate the sounds and symbols of their language into the sounds and symbols of your own language.

2. A simple way to make a new language is to start with the English alphabet and assign to each letter a different letter of the alphabet. An example follows: A=V, B=W. Thus, the entire alphabet can be used to make a code. As long as you create your language according to the rules of the code, others will be able to understand and read it.

3. A more complicated process would be to make up your own symbols and letters which you then translate back into English. Thus, ⊙ Ω ⊃ ⌝ ∫ might actually be ABCDE. Experiment before deciding what to do.

4. You may use pictures to represent the things, ideas, and experiences in your culture, so when people see the picture, they know to what it refers. An example would be a stick figure performing actions like running, jumping, sitting, and standing.

5. In the English language, letters or combinations of letters correspond to sounds that can be spoken. It is possible to make a spoken language by assigning sounds to your symbols. An example would be as follows: X = "aw," Q = "sss." It gets pretty complicated, doesn't it? Languages are very complex. Don't let that stand in your way. Remember, you are in charge of what happens in your own culture.

Exercise 35

Calculating System

Keep in mind the following items as you create your own calculating system.

1. Creating a calculating system is similar to creating a language. A code can be made with a symbol corresponding to the number 1 (1 = /, 2 = ∠), and so on, up to 10. You would stop at 10 if you wish to retain the Base-10 system of numeration that we use in our culture. Symbols standing for plus (+), minus (−), and times (×), should then be selected. Calculations would be done using the same rules that apply to our culture's calculating system.

2. If you want a greater challenge, try selecting a different base for your calculating system, such as Base 5 or Base 7. Your teacher might be able to help you find a math book that treats the base systems, enabling you to devise a system that is truly different.

3. Don't think you are limited to the symbols +, −, and ×. See if you can create an entirely different form of calculation that follows the set of rules you establish. This is your culture, where numbers calculate the way you want them to.

4. Another approach to this assignment is to learn about the calculating system devised by the Maya of Central America. They used different symbols for each number from 1 to 19 and combined these symbols to designate numbers above 19. Many ancient cultures, in addition to the Maya, used methods of numeration that could serve to stimulate your thinking. You might want to do some library research on this.

Exercise 36

Clothing

Consider the following items as you decide how to clothe the inhabitants of your new culture.

1. The clothing worn in a particular culture is made from raw materials available in that culture. Animals and birds can supply skins, wool, bones, and feathers, among other materials. Plants can supply bark, cotton, leaves, and paper. Such minerals as silver, gold, and aluminum are used in some fabrics, as well as in jewelry.

2. Many of the clothes in our culture are made from chemical processes that create entirely new fabrics. Don't hesitate to use your imagination to make up new kinds of fabrics.

3. You may be tempted to create clothing like that which already exists in our culture. Resist that temptation; you will have a much more creative product if you think in new ways.

4. Clothing design is a result of the tastes and values of the people in a culture, as well as the raw materials available. Avoid copying styles that currently exist. Consider using color combinations that are different or different fabric combinations, such as fur and cotton. Of course, if your inhabitants have three arms or huge heads, the styles will automatically be different.

5. A magazine such as *National Geographic* may give you ideas about the clothing worn by various people around the world. You might think about the way climate has helped determine the clothing people wear, and then try to discover the climate of cultures described in *National Geographic*.

Exercise 37

Resolving Differences

The following suggestions may help your group decide how to resolve disagreements with another group.

1. Whenever groups of people interact, the possibility of disagreement exists. Both groups might want the same land or the same resources, or they might disagree about the correct way to dispose of dangerous chemicals.

2. Groups of people use various ways to settle their disputes. Among the ways are the following:

   (a) Groups use force or threat of force. ("If you don't do this, we will send over our troops.")

   (b) Groups meet together and brainstorm for possible solutions. The problem gets redefined, and the groups move to a solution.

   (c) Each group gives up something it wants. We call this method *compromise*. ("If you give us the land we want, we will give you the part of the river you want.")

   (d) Both groups agree to let an entirely separate group or person (a *third party*) decide whose desires will prevail. (A judge, the United Nations, or a labor arbitrator are examples of a third party that might be used to settle a dispute.)

   (e) Sometimes groups use more than one method to resolve the dispute. (Start with compromise, move to a third-party involvement, and if that doesn't work, then resort to force.)

3. In your group, discuss what is gained and what is lost in each case when your group settles disputes with another group using force, compromise, and third-party arbitration. Then decide which method(s) appeal to you. Feel free to create entirely new ways of working out difficulties.

Exercise 38

Government

You might wish to consider the following items as you decide what kind of government your culture will use.

1. When clearly defined procedures have been established regarding who decides, how they decide, and how decisions are carried out, it is possible to classify the specific form of government a culture uses.

2. Over the centuries many forms of government have been used. Among the more common are the following:

   (a) **Monarchy:** A hereditary king or queen makes the decisions alone.

   (b) **Constitutional monarchy:** A king or queen and a group of representatives elected by the people share the responsibility for ruling together.

   (c) **Dictatorship:** A person not elected by the people is responsible for all decisions of importance. It is usual for a dictator to come from the military.

   (d) **Participatory democracy:** All important decisions are made by a majority vote of all persons affected by the decision.

   (e) **Representative democracy:** All people who wish to, vote for persons to represent them when decisions are to be made. When a majority of the representatives vote the same way, their opinion prevails.

3. See if you can supply answers to the following questions:

   (a) What form of government allows a culture to make decisions rapidly and be assured that those decisions will be followed?

   (b) What form of government allows for the most direct involvement of the people? What is its advantage?

   (c) What form of government is used where you live?

Activity 12. Focus on the Group

Introduction

In school settings, students are usually not asked to explore their interactions in groups. In this project, however, such an exploration is of vital importance. Therefore, the teacher needs to exert leadership in helping students to understand both their own communication methods and those of other members of their group.

Objectives

1. To help students learn more effective ways to work together in groups

2. To help culture groups work more effectively on their cultures

Time to complete

About five minutes for groups to fill out Exercise 39: Keeping Track of Group Work

About 10 to 15 minutes to fill out Exercise 40: Individual Assessment. The follow-up time will vary from group to group.

Materials

- Exercise 39: Keeping Track of Group Work
- Exercise 40: Individual Assessment

Procedure

1. After each group work session, have the students work together to fill out Exercise 39. Have the students return their group form to the teacher.

2. When the first section of the culture project has been completed and turned in, the teacher should explain to the class that they will be filling out a questionnaire about the way they are operating in groups. Tell students that their responses will be read by the teacher and, where appropriate, shared with their group. Emphasize that the overall intent of the questionnaire is to help each student learn how to work better in groups.

3. Each student should be given Exercise 40: Individual Assessment, and should then fill it out.

4. After the class is over, the teacher should review the comments of all culture group members and then decide upon a strategy that will assist each group to move ahead in its task.

5. During the next group meeting, the teacher should plan to meet with each group to discuss the results of the survey. Any interventions should be carried out and, if necessary, followed up in the subsequent periods.

6. Sometimes a group will have a problem serious enough to merit a meeting outside the regular class time. It is best to allow the group time to work on the problem promptly, because delay makes it more difficult to solve.

Exercise 39

Keeping Track of Group Work

Group Name _____ Date _____

Members: 1. _____   3. _____

                 2. _____   4. _____

List the work your group accomplished.

List several things you feel pleased with that your group has done.

Describe what you can do differently to accomplish more work next time.

What could the teacher do to help members of your group work more cooperatively?

Name _____ Date _____

Exercise 40

Individual Assessment

Culture Group Name _____

I find working with this group _____

_____

The things I think I do best in this group are _____

_____

When I compare my group to the other groups, I _____

_____

If I talked less than I wanted to, it was probably because _____

_____

When our group talks about our progress, I think that _____

_____

I would like some help to learn how to _____

_____

I think our group needs some help to learn how to _____

_____

Right now I feel the best about _____

_____

One thing I have learned about working in a group is _____

_____

My goals for next time are to _____

_____

Other comments I want to make are _____

_____

Activity 13. Supplemental Projects

Introduction

Unit II lends itself well to collaboration among several teachers, with activities carried out during social studies, language arts, or other classes. The basic 13 required components should serve as a starting point only, as there are many other aspects of cultures that have not been touched. Once teachers understand the project, they could create exercises that enable students to expand the ideas and concepts in their individual cultures. What follows is a brief list of some activities that could be done either in the social studies class or in the classes of collaborating teachers.

Objectives

1. To enable students to use other academic disciplines to help them develop their culture

2. To increase the opportunities for students to work cooperatively on their culture

Time to complete

This will depend entirely on the number of supplemental activities undertaken and whether the activities are conducted inside or outside the classroom.

Procedure

1. Conduct an interview with a member of a group that created a foreign culture to find out about a special invention or unique feature of that culture. Then write an article that could be sent to a local or school newspaper, describing the overall culture project and using the unique feature as an example of the kind of work being done in the culture project.

2. Write a daily journal or story describing an imaginary exploration into an unknown region of the foreign culture's territory.

3. Create short stories about events or people in that culture.

4. Write a history of the culture.

5. Create a fairy tale or tall tale that might come from that culture; then use that story to write and illustrate a book suitable for reading to a child in the first to third grade.

6. Create dances that might be done by members of that culture.

7. Make musical instruments and play music from the culture.

8. From each class, organize a meeting of representatives from all cultures. At the meeting, present them with a problem that affects all cultures. Charge the representatives with the task of solving the problem to the satisfaction of all present. These representatives should consult with the members of the culture groups they represent. All culture members should listen to the deliberations of the representatives. Possible problems could include the following:

   • One culture has recently invented a machine that could destroy all the plants in all other cultures.

   • A recent population explosion in all cultures threatens the supply of food.

   • An alien culture threatens to attack one of the represented cultures. Unfortunately, the specific threatened culture is unknown.

9. Create an evening news broadcast that would be typical of the culture's level of communication technology. Give the broadcast to other culture groups.

Activity 14. Displaying the Cultures

Introduction

Considerable work and creativity have gone into creating the culture of each group. It is important that all groups have a chance to display the cultures in one place, along with the chance to compare cultures.

Objectives

1. To encourage students to give each other feedback about their creations

2. To promote learning about each other's cultures

3. To reward group accomplishment

Time to complete

One class period to set up and one for the scavenger hunt

Materials

- Tables for display of objects
- Wall space upon which to put culture material
- Masking tape, colored markers, and poster paper

Procedure

1. Having a diversity of articles from each culture, the overall display will be impressive. Try to put the display in an area where many can see it. Walls along hallways, a large entranceway, or a special room could furnish this space. Be sure to allot enough room to each culture so that the display does not appear crowded.

2. Each group is allotted a space to display its culture, and class time is devoted to setting up the display.

3. Each group should make a large sign identifying their culture, along with the names of its members.

One activity that can familiarize students with each other's cultures is a scavenger hunt. The teacher makes up a work sheet listing at least two specific customs or features of each culture on display. Students use the work sheet to search through the available cultures for that practice or feature. Questions could be framed in the following manner: "People in _____ culture live in huts made of coconut palms."

Activity 15. Understanding Cultural Differences

Introduction

While creating their own cultures, students had to make certain choices about customs and tools. They also viewed the diverse customs of other groups. These experiences provide the basis for examining the factors that contribute to cultural diversity.

Objectives

1. To help students identify factors that contribute to cultural differences

2. To help students think about the value of having wide diversity among cultures

Time to complete

One full class period

Materials

- Exercise 41: Factors Affecting Diversity

Procedure

1. Give to each culture group one copy of Exercise 41: Factors Affecting Diversity.

2. Explain that each group should fill out the exercise together. Allow about 20 minutes for this task.

3. Choose one of the questions from the handout, and ask each group to share its answers with the class. Then help the class identify some of the common factors affecting differences—for example, weather, raw materials, values, personal tastes, physical features of the land, and available technology or scientific knowledge. Exercise 31: Factors Influencing Cultural Development should be useful in this exercise.

4. Depending on the time available, select several more questions following the same procedure. Be sure to leave about 10 minutes for the final wrap-up activity.

5. Write the following statement on the blackboard: "It is desirable that all cultures not have the same customs and values because . . . ." Have students suggest ways to finish that statement. Record the ideas on the blackboard and discuss the varying perceptions of the students.

Exercise 41

Factors Affecting Diversity

1. Explain how your new culture's location and physical features have helped in determining the following:

    (a) Food:

    (b) Transportation:

    (c) Clothing:

2. Compare your culture's technology to that of the culture in which you actually live.

3. List two facets of your culture that resulted from a compromise worked out by the members of your group.

4. Explain how some parts of your culture were shaped by the availability of certain raw materials.

5. Describe a custom in your group's culture that was borrowed from or influenced by another culture in the class.

Share Your Bright Ideas with Us!

We want to hear from you! Your valuable comments and suggestions will help us meet your current and future classroom needs.

Your name_____Date_____

School name_____Phone_____

School address_____

Grade level taught_____Subject area(s) taught_____Average class size_____

Where did you purchase this publication?_____

Was your salesperson knowledgeable about this product?   Yes_____   No_____

What monies were used to purchase this product?

____School supplemental budget   ____Federal/state funding   ____Personal

Please "grade" this Walch publication according to the following criteria:

Quality of service you received when purchasing ....A   B   C   D   F
Ease of use...A   B   C   D   F
Quality of content..A   B   C   D   F
Page layout ....A   B   C   D   F
Organization of material ....A   B   C   D   F
Suitability for grade level..A   B   C   D   F
Instructional value...A   B   C   D   F

COMMENTS:_____

_____

What specific supplemental materials would help you meet your current—or future—instructional needs?

_____

Have you used other Walch publications? If so, which ones?_____

May we use your comments in upcoming communications?   ____Yes   ____No

Please **FAX** this completed form to **207-772-3105,** or mail it to:

Product Development, J. Weston Walch, Publisher, P.O. Box 658, Portland, ME 04104-0658

We will send you a **FREE GIFT** as our way of thanking you for your feedback. **THANK YOU!**